"In *Beyond the Parentheses*, Susan guides the reader to authentically ask the questions many are snuffed from asking, including the hard ones that involve looking at self and the ego with grace. Susan uses the most powerful form of communication—storytelling—to share her personal journey so that others may lovingly begin their own journey."

—Shannon Hurd, *MA LCPC, EMDR therapist, Director of Equine Services for P.I.N.E.S.*

"Like many folks with jammed schedules, these days reading a book for fun is something I rarely get to do. The title *Beyond the Parentheses* piqued my curiosity as most books I read include science, technology, and business, primarily if it helps my new 501(c)(3) non-profit.

Susan Ford's writings gently lead the reader down the circuitous path she took in her search for understanding. What drew me in immediately were the parallels between Susan's life and mine. Was it a mere coincidence that we grew up over five hundred miles and a generation apart in completely different cultures, yet the overlapping "forced ideologies" we both encountered and endured were uncannily similar?

The more I read about her pious upbringing, the more absorbed I became in her book and in remembering my own childhood experiences with religion.

I became overly introspective after reading Susan's book and what I realized from it was not so much an understanding of religion and God but an epiphany of my own existence, my purpose in life, and the impact I have and can have on millions of others."

—DF Erbling, *MBA, Global 100 Senior Executive, Fortune 500 Tech Consultant, CEO and Executive Director of Convergence 501(c)(3)*

BEYOND THE PARENTHESES

BEYOND THE PARENTHESES

Your Journey to **Transcend** Religious Trauma, **Seek** Truth, and **Embrace** Love

SUSAN FORD

Published by Author Academy Elite
PO Box 43, Powell, OH 43065
www.AuthorAcademyElite.com

Identifiers:
LCCN: 2022909521
ISBN: 979-8-88583-078-2 (paperback)
ISBN: 979-8-88583-079-9 (hardback)
ISBN: 979-8-88583-080-5 (e-book)
Available in paperback, hardback, e-book, and audiobook

All Scripture quotations, unless otherwise indicated, are taken from the Holy Bible, King James Version (KJV). Public Domain.

Any internet addresses (websites, blogs, etc.) and telephone numbers printed in this book are offered as a resource. They are not intended in any way to be or imply an endorsement by Author Academy Elite, nor does Author Academy Elite vouch for the content of these sites and numbers for the life of this book.

Some names and identifying details have been changed to protect the privacy of individuals.

For Mr. Boyd

who inspired and encouraged me to always seek truth

"Truth and facts are always worth pursuing."

—Steven Ernest Boyd

CONTENTS

PREFACE

How would you describe your relationship with the ideas of God, the Bible, and Christianity? Complex? Non-existent? Filled with doubt, fear, anxiety, or pain? If so, you're in the right place.

This book is for you if:

- You have a complicated relationship with God and Christianity.
- You have been wounded by religion or have had faith and religious teachings used as a weapon against you.
- You believe but are filled with nagging doubts and questions.
- A part of you wants to believe but you feel like you can't.
- You identify as agnostic, atheist, deconstructing, or spiritual but not religious.

- You are navigating a return to faith after religious trauma.

The purpose of this book, and of the coaching, mentoring, and speaking work I do is to provide those harmed by religion a safe place to ask questions and explore answers so you can find truth and experience healing.

All I ask is that you bring with you the desire to understand, the willingness to listen, the vulnerability to share, and the commitment to pursue truth even if it shakes up the seemingly neat order of your current life.

So, take a deep breath. You're welcome here.

ARE YOU STUCK IN SPIRITUAL PARENTHESES?

Are the echoes of your religious past holding your spiritual future hostage?

Many of us who grew up in a church formed our initial understandings of God from an early age based on the teachings and practices of our spiritual communities.

In fundamentalist churches, too often what we learned incited fear rather than inviting love. The God we thought we knew was not someone we felt safe trusting, following, and most of all, loving.

During our time in these unhealthy churches, we racked up a collection of religious hurts, unanswered questions, and confusing experiences that formed a framework of spiritual barriers around us.

Like their literary counterparts, the spiritual barriers, or "parentheses," of harmful religious experiences and beliefs have kept and may continue to keep us trapped in their mental, emotional, and spiritual grasp, but it doesn't need to be that way.

I grew up in a church where others' understandings of God were forced upon me as irrefutable facts. Raised as a fundamentalist Baptist, I felt trapped, hopeless, and depressed until I set out to pursue truth with all my heart.

Now I'm inviting you along on a powerful journey to realize how you too can recognize, confront, and resolve lingering religious trauma, seek and pursue truth wherever it leads, then boldly embrace love and discover healing.

During this process, I will take you behind the scenes of my own journey, but you should know that *Beyond the Parentheses* is not simply a spiritual or Christian memoir for you to breeze through and place back on the shelf. The goal of sharing my path is to help ready you to walk your own. This preparation is an active, engaged process.

Before we begin, it is only fair to warn you this journey is not for everyone. It is challenging and daunting. It will keep you up at night and test the limits of your tenacity. It has the potential to radically alter the way you see the world or even the universe and your place in it. Not everyone is ready for that. *You* may not yet be ready for that, and if so, you're not alone.

In his book, *Your Secret Name*, author Kary Oberbrunner describes the rare journey of truth seeking saying, "I realized that some people aren't *ready* for the truth. Still others don't want to *hear* the truth. And only a few brave souls are willing to *pursue* the truth."

Are *you* ready?

Are *you* willing?

When you are ready and willing to pursue the truth, you will know. You will know because the idea of continuing to live your life within the status quo framework of existing limitations will be too much to bear.

As scary and intimidating as it is, you will realize your only choice is to do whatever it takes to heal, grow, and step into a truth-filled life.
Are you ready?
Are you willing?
Let's begin.

• • •

Beyond the Parentheses is divided into six parts (plus the introduction and epilogue) with reflection invites following each section. Imagine these invitations as gentle, insightful questions posed by a close friend or mentor.

If you are willing, the writing prompts are designed to guide you in identifying the thoughts, perceptions, beliefs, and feelings you hold about religion and Christianity (or whatever faith tradition you have spent time in).

Once you have answered the prompts, you can then process your answers and gain insight from them. Along the way, you may come to better realize how past religious experiences have framed your present spiritual views.

I invite you first to read each part of the book. Then, to get the most value out of this exercise, fill in the blanks of the reflection questions with the first thing that comes to mind. You are not looking for the filtered, "socially acceptable" or "right" answers. This is not a job interview or online dating screening.

The writing prompt process is for your self-awareness and growth, so respond to each prompt honestly and vulnerably. The best answer is the one that is true for you even if you wish the answer were something else. This journey is about pursuing truth, so let's start by being truthful with ourselves.

Re-read and consider your answers later once you have completed the full set of questions for each part. Journaling is an excellent way to explore your responses as well as the emotions, thoughts, and memories that go with them.

If you have a counselor, mentor, or spiritual advisor you trust, consider sharing some of your thoughts with them so they can offer insight and perspective as my confidants did for me.

Finally, remember just because it's a personal journey, that doesn't mean you walk alone. I'll be right here, encouraging you along the way.

With love,

Susan

Reflection Invite: Introduction

1. I have been held back in my spiritual life by _____
   _____
   _____
   _____
   _____.

   The effect this had on me was _____
   _____
   _____
   _____
   _____.

2. I want to transcend that barrier/those barriers because
   _____
   _____
   _____
   _____
   _____.

3. This journey is important to me because _____
   _____
   _____
   _____
   _____
   _____.

4. As I prepare for this experience, my biggest fear is

_____

_____

_____

and my greatest hope is _____

_____

_____

_____.

5. I feel _____
about facing my religious past.

PART 1
LIVING UNDER LEGALISM

We are all a product of our upbringing, and
our beliefs reflect our experiences.

—Megan Phelps-Roper

CHAPTER 1
IN THE BEGINNING

We each have distinct barriers to personal faith. For me, these first spiritual roadblocks took the shape of the legalistic fundamentalist Baptist church in which I was raised from the time I was eight years old. Its unique paradigm permeated and shaped my spiritual worldview in lasting ways.

I was born on a Thursday, and three days later, on that very first Sunday, I was in church. I know this because growing up, my parents often told me the story. They spoke of it as though it were a badge of honor and pride—like having the county's first New Year's baby or something. It was their very first act as Christian parents. At not even a week old, they had begun to "train up their child in the way she should go," just as Proverbs 22:6 instructed.

Three days old, and figuratively speaking, my butt was already in the pew, to use one of my dad's favorite phrases. My freshly diapered butt was actually strapped in a car seat placed underneath the pew, but still, I was there, hearing the Word.

Starting that day, through the first eighteen years of my life, I can count on both hands the number of Sundays we missed church. Even when we were traveling on vacation, there was no problem. Simply pick a Baptist church from the handy local phone book found in the hotel nightstand next to the Gideon Bible.

On any given Sunday, we were there, butts in our unofficially reserved pew, for both Sunday school and church service. There was also a Sunday evening service, but we never attended it.

As I understood it, that service seemed to be reserved for the pastor's family, who had no choice but to attend, and for elderly parishioners who had nowhere to be early the following morning. We had school, and Dad had work, so apparently, God forgave our absence.

● ● ●

The church I attended from birth to eight years old was affiliated with what was then known as the Baptist General Conference (BGC). In 2008, as part of a rebranding effort—and perhaps to distance itself from the stigma of rigid intolerance often associated with fundamental Baptist congregations—the BGC renamed itself "Converge."

My memories of this first church are mainly vague and unremarkable. I do fondly recall the senior pastor who was a genuinely loving, grandfatherly man. He held a special place in his heart for children. He would bring us up to sit on the stage at the front of the church with him while he told us stories.

At Christmas time, he gifted each of the children in the congregation little presents, decorated a beautiful tree in the sanctuary, and coordinated the Christmas pageant. He lit up with love whenever he interacted with us, and I liked him and his wife very much.

When I was eight years old, we left that church as part of a congressional split driven by irreconcilable differences between certain parishioners and the new pastor.

I was, of course, too young at the time to be involved in the decision-making process, but as the situation escalated, I remember listening to my parents discuss their options on the drive home from church each Sunday.

They wanted to avoid the drama of the whole unraveling mess as much as possible and to be part of a stable, functional congregation rather than getting caught up in the infighting.

The new pastor was in favor of cutting cherished youth programs and outreach activities which my parents believed in. Other parishioners who disagreed with the direction the main church body was taking were already seeking out greener pastures.

Finally, my dad, a local service station owner, came home one night to announce the new pastor of another local church had stopped in to get his vehicle repaired. The pastor and my dad had hit it off, and Dad decided we would join the exodus. We would move to the new church in a neighboring town.

At the time, I don't remember being overly concerned about the move, and I really expected my experience at the new church to be much the same as it had been at the one we were leaving.

One Door and Only One

At both our original and our new church, songs were an important part of worship services and youth group meetings. Beyond offering the welcome chance to stand up and stretch your legs, they were a way to glorify and praise God or to encourage acts like participation in an altar call for the confession of sins.

Children started learning classic songs like "Jesus Loves Me" from the time they could speak. In my family, we had to sing that song before bed each night, at least until I was in middle school and my parents quit trying to force the issue of nightly family devotionals.

In the morning, on our way to the school bus, my mom would lead my sister and me in singing "This Is the Day That the Lord Has Made."

Though I would later come to dislike both these songs after having to sing them daily, as a little girl, I remember liking "Jesus Loves Me" along with "Jesus Loves the Little Children," "He's Got the Whole World in His Hands," and other songs that focused on the roles of Jesus and God as loving, caring beings who wanted the best for us and who were there to nurture and protect us.

Around my third birthday, I was introduced to the song "One Door and Only One." Now, I should preface this next part with a bit of backstory. According to my mother, I began talking incredibly early and was speaking in full sentences with an understanding of past, present, and future tenses by the age of eighteen months.

I share this because, looking back, I imagine the other three-year-old children who learned this song alongside me were not affected by it in the same way or to nearly the same extent. They simply heard the singsong tune and parroted back the words without ever really internalizing them and understanding their deeper meaning. To them, it was just another song.

For me, it was life-altering.

The song has three short verses, although we often sang just the first. It speaks of there being one door with two sides. A person can be either on the inside or outside of this single door—a metaphor for belief and acceptance of Jesus' death and resurrection as an atonement for our sins. The song then asks which side of the door we each are on.

I don't remember the exact conversation, but my mother later recounted how I had come to her, concerned, after learning this song. I solemnly told her, "You and Daddy are on the inside."

"Yes," she agreed.

"And I am on the outside."

Again, she nodded in the affirmative.

"I want to be on the inside too!" I announced.

She led me through a version of the "sinner's prayer," whereby one acknowledges their inability to live a sinless life and their need for a perfect savior to atone for their sins.

The person praying the prayer indicates a belief in and acceptance of Jesus Christ as said savior. The prayer typically ends with asking Jesus to come into your heart and change your life.

I prayed that prayer and then proudly proclaimed, "Now I'm on the inside!"

My mother and father were thrilled. Their daughter had reached the age of accountability and "made a decision for Christ" at the tender age of three. It was a moment of great rejoicing for them.

As I reflect on this moment, over thirty years later, my emotions are far less singular. I do not share my parents' pure unbridled enthusiasm. In fact, the scene still troubles me. Yes, I do believe that "born again" experience was genuine, and my belief at that time was real, but I also see a young girl who had just been told by an authority figure that she was going to be permanently separated from her mommy and daddy unless she decided to follow Jesus.

What three-year-old would choose to be abandoned and alone, forever cut off from her primary caregivers? Naturally, I chose Christianity.

There is an ongoing debate in Christian circles about the concept of the "age of accountability" and what that age might be.

The basic questions at the root of the issue are these:

- At what point are children treated the same as adults when it comes to the judgment of their souls?
- What are the criteria that determine when children must accept Jesus or risk going to Hell if they die as opposed to getting a free pass to Heaven?
- Is the so-called age of accountability a single set age that applies to all children, or is it based on intellectual capacity and the ability to understand and process the information being presented?

The debate stems from the fact that the Bible does not specifically lay out the age of accountability or even reference the term at all. Indeed, each denomination cites different verses or precedents as justification for their stance on the topic.

The complexity of the issue aside, for me, the reality was that at a very young age, I had already been introduced to the fear of Hell. I understood enough of the message to know I was being told if I did not believe in Jesus as my savior, I would forever be separated from the two people I loved and needed most—my mommy and daddy.

So, I made a choice.

I still wonder how much of that choice was seated in the religious fear that would partner with its friend, religious guilt, and come to define my understanding of the character of God and his relationship with humanity.

Fundamentalism, Legalism, and Pietism

Stick with me for a moment because, while I'm not a theologian, to tell my story, I need to use terms like fundamental, fundamentalism, legalism, pietism, and more.

These words come to us baked in centuries of history, tradition, and controversy. Their uses have shifted over time, and application is often a matter of personal perspective and opinion. Today, one person's legalistic fundamentalist church can be another person's middle-of-the-road evangelical congregation.

This means that before I can get back into my story, I proactively need to clear up potential misunderstanding by sharing how I'm going to use these loaded labels.

In this book, fundamental churches and fundamental Christians are those whose statements of faith include the following as fundamentals (or non-negotiable truths and requirements) of the Christian faith:

- A belief in the Bible as the inerrant word of God
- A literal interpretation of scriptures
- The virgin birth
- The Trinity
- The deity of Christ
- Salvation by grace through faith
- One way to salvation through acceptance of the substitutionary death and resurrection of Jesus.

As I'm applying these labels, churches and believers can be fundamental without being fundamentalist.

Fundamental believers and churches cross into fundamentalism when not only do they hold to the non-negotiable importance of the items on the above list, but they include other beliefs— like, for example, the sole use of specific translations of the Bible, a policy of no contemporary worship music, or women not being in positions of church leadership—as equally important and non-negotiable requirements for genuine Christianity rather than making them secondary or tertiary points of doctrine.

A legalistic church can be recognized by its leadership's heavy-handed use of biblical law to regulate and direct the actions of the congregation. Law and gospel may be preached together, or sometimes law is even preached *as* gospel.

When this happens, members of a legalistic church find themselves still living under the letter of the law plus additional specific manmade rules, though as believers they were freed by the gospel.

Even situations that would usually be left up to each believer to decide based on the use of spiritual discernment are instead regulated by the pastor. He decides this is the way our church operates and so this is what we do—this is what we *all* do—whether it is laid out that way in the Bible or not.

My sister put it perfectly when she summarized the legalistic mindset as, "If it's not clearly stated in the Bible that it's right, it must be wrong."

Legalism can be subtle and hard to identify in some churches because it is not always so much the beliefs and values that are wrong as it is the tactics and strategies used to enforce those beliefs. For example, there is obviously nothing biblically wrong with attending church. Meeting with those who share your faith is a God-directed action. The problem is that a legalistic church may keep track of how often members attend then chastise and shame those who have missed a service or two.

In a legalistic church, the pastor's assumption often seems to be that members of his congregation are lazy Christians who do not want to be godly on their own and must therefore be continuously goaded into it through threatening fear-driven sermons on the law. The stereotypical "fire and brimstone" style of preaching is prevalent even if the entire congregation is made up of believers. The theory seems to be that correct behavior will create belief versus belief inspiring behavior.

Believers who attend a legalistic church often learn to be pietistic as well. While piety is a state of reverence and a worshipful attitude toward God, pietism is marked by an intense introspective focus and continual hyper analysis of our actions, thoughts, and feelings for God.

As pietists in a legalistic, fundamentalist church, we hyper analyze everything about ourselves then compare it to the list of spiritual rules and regulations we have been given. When our actions or our emotions surrounding those actions inevitably fail to live up to the standard, we berate ourselves for failing. We quietly come to the fear-filled pietistic conclusion that we may not be "true Christians" after all.

We internalize all this spiritual trauma, resolving to try harder to prove ourselves, and so the cycle repeats until it chews us up and spits us out or we walk away.

Legalistic Fundamentalism in Action

The church we moved to when I was eight identified itself as an Independent Fundamental Baptist (IFB) church, although it was affiliated with the General Association of

Regular Baptist Churches (GARBC). Its website currently lists it as "an evangelical, conservative, Baptist church."

Not all IFB churches are fundamentalist, legalistic, and/or pietistic at their core, but during the time that my family attended it, this church and its congregation displayed all such tendencies.

Within my fundamentalist church, legalism abounded, giving us plenty of rules to learn and adhere to from an early age.

We read only the King James Version (KJV)[1] of the Bible, and we sang solely traditional songs from the hymnals accompanied by a piano and organ (no percussion instruments). Musical performances were followed by an "amen," but no clapping lest we glorify man, not God. Only men could be pastors, deacons, and leaders of co-ed adult study groups, though women could teach children's church, lead women's groups, and, of course, work in the nursery.

A 10% tithe was expected as was weekly attendance of Sunday morning bible school and church service (as noted before, Sunday evening service was indeed optional at our church). Participation in Wednesday youth group or prayer meeting plus an additional weekly small group Bible study were strongly encouraged.

These rules existed to ensure we followed the path our church elders had laid out for us, and we did not deviate or dangerously lean unto our own understanding.

To be clear and fair, let me reiterate that I don't believe all the lessons taught and sermons preached were "wrong" per se. The pastors supported their teachings using numerous Bible verses alongside personal stories and analogies.

Many of the shifts from fundamental to fundamentalist and from being grounded in biblical truth to drifting into legalism were subtle. The pastors may not have even realized they were instilling a pietistic rather than a reverent mindset in their church members.

For someone like me, however, the impact was drastic. Although an outsider may have recognized the flags of legalistic fundamentalism, at the time, the culture within this church was all that I knew. It was my normal.

The Danger of Separatism

A strong separatist doctrine is prevalent within most fundamental churches (whether fundamentalistic and legalistic or not), and a key shared feature of IFB churches is that they only associate with other IFB churches who share their beliefs on all the doctrinal points that are considered fundamental.

For example, the current statement of faith for the IFB church we used to attend reads in part:

> "We believe in obedience to the Biblical commands to separate entirely from worldliness and ecclesiastical apostasy, unto God. This separation involves…ecclesiastical separation from churches that are not fundamental, independent, Bible believing congregations…"

An IFB church that has drifted into fundamentalism can consider so many points to be fundamental to the faith that any other church deemed acceptable to associate with will look identical right down to the legalistic details and pietistic mindset. Church members miss the opportunity to interact with Christians who hold even a slightly different perspective on any point of biblical interpretation or the details of Christian life.

For example, IFB churches will not even associate with other Baptist churches who have joined one of the Baptist conferences of churches because said affiliated churches are no longer independent.

• • •

Fundamentalism, legalism, and pietism are all normalized and reinforced in such a church, so those of us who grew up in this environment truly had no concept of anything else. For a child who is born blind, it is normal not to see. For a child with congenital deafness, it is normal not to hear. A child who is raised to be a legalistic, pietistic, fundamentalist knows no different. Their paradigm cannot change until they later learn from an outside source that there are other perspectives and nuanced variations of belief they were never exposed to.

As child fundamentalists, our worldview and self-image were warped and contorted by this legalistic belief system until, like a deformed tree, we grew to be dependent, leaning on the altar of pietism for support.

The strict regulations and legalistic tenets of fundamentalism permeated our delicate psyches at a critical time as we were forming our understanding of life. We internalized them, and they became a part of us in ways we would not consciously realize until much later.

CHAPTER 2
TRAIN UP A CHILD

As anyone who was raised in the Bible Belt knows, Wednesday night is a church night. Some schools purposely do not schedule extracurricular events on Wednesdays simply to avoid the inevitable conflict with Catholic catechism courses and Protestant youth group meetings.

Like many Baptist and other Protestant churches, both the first church we attended and the one we moved to when I was eight years old had a version of a youth group called the AWANA program.

AWANA, an acronym for "Approved Workmen Are Not Ashamed," derives its name from a verse in Second Timothy: "Study to shew thyself approved unto God, a workman that needeth not to be ashamed, rightly dividing the word of truth" (2 Timothy 2:15).

The two-hour-a-week program was designed for kids ranging from three years old through seniors in high school. My parents got involved with it shortly before I was born and then spent more than thirty-three years as AWANA leaders, having also been joint club commanders in charge of the whole program in our church several times during their tenure.

In the AWANA program, each age range is part of its own unique club within a club. The youngest group, and the one I started out in, is called Cubbies. The Cubbies theme song talks about being "happy all day long" and knowing that "Jesus is a friend to us. He loves each girl and boy."

In Cubbies, we played games, sang songs, and were taught basic biblical stories like the days of creation and about the animals getting on Noah's ark two-by-two.

At age five or six, depending on when the child goes to kindergarten, a Cubbie moves into the Sparks program. In this age group, the message behind the most popular songs morphs from restful loving security to more action-oriented themes like "Give Me Oil in My Lamp" and "This Little Light of Mine." These songs shift the focus to actions the young believer is expected to take including evangelism as a means of publicly proving and sharing their faith.

The emphasis on evangelism isn't just for song time. One of the first few "sections" a Sparkie must pass in their shiny new handbook is called "invite a friend." Unless an alternate activity is requested and approved, each clubber is required to go out and convince an "unchurched" friend to come to AWANA with them. Once said friend attends an AWANA club meeting, the Sparkie can move on with memorizing Bible verses and earning more little press-in jewels to adorn the plastic crown that is pinned onto their bright red version of a Girl Scout vest.

By including the invite a friend section in every handbook for clubbers in kindergarten through junior high, the creators of the AWANA program all but ensured its growth and the continued development of young children into miniature disciples who would go out spreading the word of God to the masses by whatever means necessary.

It wasn't easy though. In a small school district with a limited pool of students to choose from, even if you weren't already a frequent target of bullying like I was, the mandate to bring a friend to club represented a logistical problem. Each year you had to bring someone new to pass the section. You couldn't simply get the person who attended one meeting last year to come back one more time this year. Eventually you ran out of "unchurched" kids in your class who were willing to be railroaded into club attendance or whose parents were inclined to send them off for the night, if only so they could enjoy an evening of free childcare.

To top it off, it was deeply uncomfortable to be forced to coerce a classmate into attending a religious event where you and the other self-righteous "church kids" would look on smugly while the club leaders pitched the salvation message and worked to sell the would-be clubber on returning the following week.

It still seems to me that by continuing to include the "invite a friend" section in each handbook, the AWANA program designers promote an awkwardly distasteful sort of forced and artificial children-targeted "witnessing" with results measured in quantifiable metrics that would make pietists proud.

● ● ●

In addition to memorizing Bible verses and getting others to attend, the AWANA program reserved segments of the night for games, Bible lessons, and singing. As co-commander, my dad oversaw both the games and singing.

AWANA games were generally structured in a track and field format. We competed in relay races with batons, three-legged races (one of my favorites), bean bag tosses, and all sorts of other fun games.

I hated gym class, where I was always picked last or second to last due to my non-existent popularity status coupled with my equally negligible hand-eye coordination, but I did like the competitive nature of AWANA game time, especially when it involved floor hockey or something else in which I could be the best.

The song part had some entertaining songs mixed in with others that I found vaguely disturbing at the time and more questionable now looking back.

We would sing the "I'm in the Lord's Army" song rife with lyrics about how we may never be in the actual military, but we were in the Lord's Army. "Yes, sir!" we barked out like true basic training recruits as we rendered a haphazard and ill-timed salute. The song's child indoctrination elements are to me reminiscent of German youth singing and saluting in the 1930s, only much less organized.

The AWANA theme song itself also had some military imagery and child indoctrination-type lyrics like, "Boys and girls for his service claimed," "Hail AWANA on the march for youth!" and "We'll fight victorious for Christ our King. Youth—on the march!"

Another popular selection, "Happy All the Time (Inright, Outright)," modeled for us that "since Jesus Christ came in and cleansed my heart from sin, I'm inright, outright, upright, downright happy all the time."

Given my pietistic upbringing, what I gleaned from these lyrics was that if at any time I was not 100% ecstatically happy, clearly, I must be doing something wrong as a Christian. I just needed to try harder, get better, and hide all evidence of failure in the meantime least anyone notice and question my status as a child of God.

We Are the Champions

One of the most pivotal events of the entire AWANA year was the Saturday of Bible Quizzing. Think Bible Jeopardy for kids from fourth through eighth grade, complete with ribbons, trophies, medals, and plenty of praise for the victors.

I have an extremely competitive nature, so I was always wanting to be the best and striving to achieve an unattainable level of perfection. I was also a total nerd who had been trained in the art of memorization since I started the AWANA Cubbies program at three years old.

As a six-year-old Sparkie, I had to memorize all the books of the Bible and recite them in order. Words like "Ecclesiastes" and "Thessalonians" are tongue twisters at any age, but my mom drilled me and drilled me on those sections, coming up with catchy limericks and memorization techniques. I eventually passed the section and still retain the random ability to list all the books of the Bible in under twenty seconds.

By the time I reached fourth grade and started taking part in Bible quizzing, I had streamlined my ability to memorize blocks of text and vast quantities of information then sift through it quickly for the correct answer.

As a case in point, when I was in sixth grade, I played Charles Dickens' niece Helen in *A Christmas Carol*. I memorized the entire script verbatim and would cue any of my fellow actors if they missed a line. Thankfully, they were all adults who were wonderfully patient with my emerging need to show off and prove my worth.

We trained for Bible quizzing as if it were the Olympics. For the two months before the event, Saturdays were reserved for serious practice. My mom, our coach, provided us with sample paddles so we could practice selecting the correct multiple-choice answer, pulling it out, and holding it up for the proctor to check. We trained to press our buzzers as soon as we could tell where a fill-in-the-blank question was going so we would beat the other teams with our lightning speed. For the group answer part, we worked on speaking softly and sitting in a circle facing each other so our competitors would not be able to read our lips or hear the answer we were discussing. It was exhilarating, and all our training paid off when we took first place nearly every year.

One of the five years I quizzed, there were no other clubbers my age in the church. Rather than admit defeat and not compete, I asked to go alone. Teams usually consisted of four people, with two at a time being involved in the multiple-choice or buzzer portions and the whole team taking part in the team answer section. This put me at an unavoidable disadvantage since each participant could only be on stage for fifty percent of the multiple-choice and the buzzer questions. Since there was no one to take my place during the other half of the questions, my team would earn no points in those segments. Undaunted, I racked up as many points as possible during my time on stage. I finished in second place ahead of several full four-person teams.

It was intense, it was competitive, and I loved it. Of course, I loved it for all the wrong reasons. It was not about learning more and developing a relationship with God. It was externally motivated by winning, being the best, doing everything that was expected of me, and showing everyone that I was as close as I could be to the top of the legalistic Christian perfection pedestal.

A Week in the Life

As a high-achieving AWANA clubber, I was part of an army of children on fire for God, and there was nothing we could not do in his name. This was on Wednesday night. On Thursday, I got ridiculed and bullied in school. On Friday, I screwed up the courage to invite (read: beg) someone to attend AWANA next week—their parents said yes when my mom sweetened the deal by throwing in free dinner and chauffeur service. Saturday, I had a bit of a reprieve, although too often, like many kids I failed to clean my room or do laundry, and so got in trouble for it. Bright and early Sunday morning, I was back at church in a pew listening to a sermon about being a lukewarm Christian and how God hated lukewarm Christians and spat them out of his mouth.

Maybe that was just the reality of life in the trenches as a child warrior of God, but there was a disconnect between the concept of being a victorious fighter on Wednesday night, a bullied kid on Thursday and Friday, a lazy daughter on Saturday, and a pathetic, lukewarm excuse for a Christian on Sunday.

It felt like an exhausting constantly revolving hamster wheel of rules, expectations, and failures to hide.

Church Kid Summer

The AWANA club was only in session during the school year, but that did not mean the summer lacked religious events for children. We church kids attended Vacation Bible School (VBS) and church camp instead.

VBS was a week-long youth event geared for and pitched to kids who had attended AWANA during the school year. Of course, we were also incentivized to go out and recruit as many unchurched kids as possible. The attendees on day one of VBS were divided into two teams, and the team that had the most total attendees with butts in seats by the final day would win an ice cream party.

The one-to-two-week camps at the Christian college a few hours from home were themed—"Native American" for fourth through sixth grades and either sports or music for middle school. So yes, I did technically go to band camp, but it was nothing like the stereotypical secular band camp experience some people chuckle about.

Sleeping in the big teepees at "Native American" camp was something to look forward to, though for an introvert, sharing the space with nine other girls and a camp counselor for a week was draining.

The food was fairly good other than the fact that no one knew how to toast marshmallows as perfectly as my dad had taught me.

When Dad prepared marshmallows, he held the fork over a nice bed of coals—not flames—patiently waiting until it was just golden brown, then rotating it again, slowly and precisely like a spit. The result was a slightly crisp golden skin and a fluffy, gooey melted interior.

At camp, I was horrified to see everyone just plunge their marshmallows directly into the flames. They waited for the sugary treats to catch fire, let them incinerate, then blew out the flame and ate the resultant nasty charcoal mess that was black on the outside and raw on the inside. No, thank you—that was not a marshmallow!

The fourth through sixth grade campers had two mandatory hour-and-a-half-long church services each day plus a devotional time with our teepee's counselor each night.

Some of the sermons were geared toward the non-believers in the crowd, and these I listened to with a sense of relief and knowing superiority. I was safe in the knowledge that I had already checked that box and didn't have to take what I viewed as deeply embarrassing public walk down the aisle to make a confession of faith.

Many of the other sermons, in their zealous efforts to drive spiritual growth, focused on the ways we as young Christians were likely failing to live up to God's ideal vision and plan. These messages felt to me like another criticism and guilt-inducing confirmation of my unacceptable spiritual shortcomings.

Regardless, as head deacon's daughters, Karen and I believed we shouldn't respond to altar calls because that would be a sign of weakness and flaws. It would reflect badly on us and our church.

Those calls were for other people who needed help, and we were glad they could get the help they needed. We were simply there to support the flawed sinners who weren't right with God like we perfect young Pharisees-in-training were.

I looked forward instead to the other activities like swimming, the water slide, paddle boats, bonfires, and trips to the little on-site store for souvenirs and ice cream.

What You Wear Matters

Being at a conservative Christian college, the camp had strict dress codes. Shorts had to be knee-length, and no tank tops were allowed. We girls had to wear both a t-shirt and knee-length shorts over our one-piece swimsuits so the sight of our female bodies would not cause our male campmates to stumble in their walk with God.

It reminded me of the swim dresses I had read about Victorian women wearing, only more hodge-podge and significantly less stylish. It may have been good practice for not drowning in case you ever got thrown off a boat fully clothed, but it was not so much fun to just go to the beach in. Of course, it did cut back on the amount of sunblock I needed to slather all over my very white Finnish skin.

This sort of very conservative dress is common in fundamental communities. I don't recall what church we were visiting when I first saw the girls and women wearing tasteful, fashionable clothing, but I do remember my reaction. I arrogantly assumed they could not possibly be Christians. Part of being a Christian woman, at least the way I had received the message, was to dress in an outdated, frumpy, conservative way at church so as not to cause any male Christians to stumble.

Where I came from, anyone who didn't follow all the rules was suspect. Our pianist's older teenage daughter wore more modern dresses and even dared to wear black dress pants on occasion. No midriff or excessive cleavage was showing, and the dress hems were just a few inches above her knees, but I was certain she was going to Hell. Me on the other hand? My pious collection of below-the-knee and floor-length gowns with their appropriately high necklines and loose fit would keep me in good standing with God.

Overly modest dress wasn't touted as a means to salvation in my church, but rather as an external indicator of your soul's status. Shirts that were too fitted or shorts that were too short could be a sign that you weren't really saved, because what true Christian would dress that way?

A Different Kind of Band Camp

Middle school band camp included just one church service a day, though with more high-stakes guilt-inducing messaging since we were at the age where we might look at the other sex inappropriately or commit some other more critical sin than we were prone to in our younger years.

The camp I attended as a fifteen-year-old was an all-inclusive music camp, so I played the clarinet in the band and sang soprano in the choir. The nice thing about participating in both band and choir was there had to be plenty of time devoted to learning the music and practicing throughout the week, which left little time to cram in too many extra church services.

At camp, I felt trapped, imprisoned, and forced to go along with everything because there was no other choice. I was not there of my own volition, but I also hadn't verbally protested. As a deacon's daughter, I knew the expectations. I had to set a good example for others.

My parents attended the final band camp concert and made a recording of it which my mother and I watched recently as I was transferring family movies from VHS to MP4. She commented on how unhappy I looked.

"You really hated it there, didn't you?" she observed sadly.

My pain at having to sing the words that I was no longer sure I believed was clearly visually evident on the recording.

Advantages of Growing up Fundie

Though the underlying sense of my experience growing up in the fundamentalist church was negative, it wasn't all bad.

One of the positives I take with me from that time is learning how to read sheet music from an early age. Initially, I would simply sing the melody with everyone else, but later I learned to harmonize a bit. It was good practice, and it set me up to excel in both band and choir at school.

Music also provided a means of connecting with my father at church. He was the song leader for just about every youth event—AWANA, VBS, and Christmas caroling at the local nursing homes.

Everyone gravitated toward the upbeat enthusiasm and charisma he brought to the act of singing. I especially remember the songs like "I am a C (C-H-R-I-S-T-I-A-N)" that were designed to be repeated over and over, speeding up each time until most of the singers were tripping over the words and could no longer keep up. The singing ended with all the kids dissolving into fits of giggles.

My dad and I would always get the furthest. As the tempo picked up and everyone else began to fall out, we would sing louder and with even more enthusiasm. His eyes crinkled up and caught mine, twinkling with mischievousness as we barreled through to the end of the verse.

We did not often connect in my older childhood and teen years, but in those shared moments of frantic song, I felt his love and pride.

Also, it turns out, hearing, reading, and memorizing Bible verses in only KJV from the time you are a toddler does set you up with certain linguistic advantages. I grew up with an intimate familiarity with the usage of antiquated words like "thee, thou, hither, whither, unto, whence" and many others.

I did not fully realize what an advantage this was until our high school English class began reading Shakespeare, and my Lutheran best friend, Beth, and I had no problems understanding the flowery language and complex sentence structures that confounded many others.

CHAPTER 3
DROWNING IN DOGMA

"Susan, stop being so dramatic!" My parents told me that often starting from the time I was about four years old. When I was eight, my mom remembers them looking at one another and saying, "Well, maybe we should channel all that drama."

They took me to auditions for our local theater's production of the musical *Cinderella*, and I fell in love with the stage. I performed in a dozen local shows throughout my elementary school and high school years.

I was Wendy, exploring Never Land and being saved by Peter Pan. I was Snow White finding her prince. I was one of the orphans Daddy Warbucks adopted alongside Annie. I was Charles Dickens' niece, Helen, whom he loved and protected.

Although I did not recognize it at the time, looking back, I see that some of my favorite roles were those in which my character was cared for and valued. She was herself, and she was loved for it.

I do not mean to say my parents did not love me because they truly did, and still do. As an adult, I can better see the complexities of it. The challenges they faced as Christian parents in general were amplified as parents who were leaders in a legalistic, fundamentalist church. If I thought the bar was set high for me as a head deacon's daughter, I can only imagine the intensity of the standards my mom and dad were held to.

● ● ●

From an early age, I consciously recognized many of the things expected of me as a good upstanding Christian girl and a deacon's daughter.

Among other things, I understood that I was to show up to church every Sunday wearing a dress. I was to take part actively in Sunday school and to sit silently and attentively during the church service. I was to memorize the Bible and witness to others. I was to turn the other cheek when I was bullied at school. I was to honor my father and mother.

I believed I was to accept blindly and internalize readily all the teachings of my pastor, Sunday school teachers, youth group leaders, and parents because those adults were the God-given authority figures in my life.

This emphasis on meeting authority figures' expectations extended outside of church as well. I was to get excellent grades in school—I was told more than once that the A-minus I brought home was not good enough, and I could have done better.

In short, I believed I needed to be perfect. There was no room for questions, no room for debate or uncertainty, no room for independent thought—only simple, unwavering, and obedient perfection.

Since the religious environment I was raised in did not value critical thought, my intensely independent thoughts, ideas, feelings, and questions likely challenged my parents. I knew they loved me, yet I also felt they loved the version of me who fit the church's mold and expectations best. It was easier, safer, and less likely to cause them trouble.

Over time, I learned that the "self" I showed to the world needed to meet parental and church expectations. My feelings could be explored and processed through theater where they weren't viewed as being "over-dramatic," but rather simply the hallmarks of a good actress. If I did this, I was safe. I was lovable.

Hiding Behind a Mask

In ancient Japan, stage actors adopted a series of special face coverings called Noh masks to enhance their pantomime and dance performances. The Noh masks were carefully crafted to hide the performer's own face and instead portray a face with a neutral expression. Was the character wearing the mask sad? Was he happy? Was he angry? The mask revealed nothing. It was only through the body language of the performer and the tilting of the mask that the audience was able to interpret the emotional state of the character.

Geishas also practice the art of turning their faces into a sort of living Noh mask. An apprentice geisha, resplendent in her brightly colored, embroidered silk kimono, perched atop towering Okobo shoes, her face painted a stark white with miniature crimson lips, is a piece of living artwork. She has become a character for her clients to interact with, her expression giving nothing of her inner life away. She is as they wish and imagine her to be—whatever that is.

Like the Japanese Noh masks and the carefully rehearsed geisha's visage, when I became a teenager, I redoubled my efforts to outwardly present what my church and parents wanted to see. I focused on keeping my normally very expressive face purposefully neutral and studiously worked on developing the safety of my mask.

Emotional vulnerability was not safe in my family or church. I had already learned exposing my feelings was dangerous. They would not be understood, but merely labeled and written off as irrelevant or contrived. It was best to stuff those feelings down inside as much as possible while outwardly portraying what was expected of me.

I took this task on without knowing how difficult it would ultimately become.

Living in the End Times

My parents enjoy traveling, and they wanted my sister Karen and me to have the opportunity to see as much of the country as possible. During our annual two-week family road trip, Karen and I crammed into the backseat of our creamy white Oldsmobile with a maroon Coleman cooler supplying the neutral territory between us. We propped our pillows on top of the cooler, continually jockeying for more real estate on which to nap in between the memorable sightseeing adventures.

Sometimes I wrapped the pillow around my head or wore headphones in a futile attempt to block out the incessant chatter of the radio.

My dad rarely listened to the radio at home, but the long hours of our summer road trips were punctuated by a steady stream of talk shows and commentary on the Voice of Christian Youth America station.

The experts on these talk shows seemed to share my father's grim outlook on the state of the world and the immediate prospects for humanity. They were acutely certain we were living in the End Times. It was a simple reality that permeated their worldview and outlook on life. Their sentiments aligned with the equally depressing Book of Revelation inspired messages that often rained down from our church's pulpit on Sundays. Christians will suffer, they will die, and life will be miserable, but Jesus will come very soon, any day now, so be sure to share the "good news" with others, that they too may have the privilege of suffering for their faith. (That was in the late '90s when certain sects touted the pre-Y2K return of Jesus.)

While my father spoke about the second coming with great anticipation, Jesus' imminent return was a source of sorrow and grief for me since, based on the information I was being given, I might not live past the age of thirteen.

Others who were raised in similar conservative Christian faiths write of experiencing fear during thunderstorms as they thought one of the loud thunderclaps could be heralding Christ's return.

In my case, the anxiety manifested on cloudy days in moments when the clouds would part, and a particularly bright beam of light would shine through.

Although I knew I was supposed to be laying up my treasures in Heaven, what I had heard of Heaven sounded unappealing. I envisioned it as something akin to being stuck in church or church camp all day.

We would receive bejeweled crowns for the good works we had done and the souls we had led to Christ, but we would be expected to give them all back again anyway to show our gratitude. There would be many church sermons, and we would each have our own mansion to walk to on golden streets.

It sounded cold, sterile, and lonely. I didn't want to live in a huge house all alone no matter how opulent it was. What I wanted was to be able to grow up, to have my first kiss, and to marry a man who loved me, someone who would nurture and protect me. He would view me as a worthy life partner, not a submissive doormat to wipe his feet on.

I wanted time to discover who I was meant to become in this life and how I could make a difference doing something that mattered. I wanted to have children and nurture them lovingly in a safe place where they could grow up surrounded by beauty and peace.

Those were my dreams, yet with each End Times sermon and talk show message I heard, it seemed less and less likely I would ever have the chance to fulfill them.

I felt cheated, bitter, and increasingly depressed. As high school and the end of the world approached, I stopped planning my life and doing anything to further those seemingly pointless dreams for a future that would likely never come.

The Most Depressing Day of the Week

According to Crisis Text Line data, Sunday is the most depressing day of the week for teens.[2] For some, this may be due to apprehension about the upcoming school week, but for me, Sunday was the melancholiest day because I had to wake up early to go be trapped in a pew while the pastor preached messages that incited fear and removed hope. His words picked at the implied shortcomings of the congregation as they held us up to an impossible standard.

Salvation may have been through faith, but good works and living a perfect Christian life for others to see were important ways to "demonstrate fruit" and prove to yourself and others that you really were saved. If at any point you were found to be missing the mark, your very salvation could be considered up for debate.

The team of pastors at the *Theocast* podcast[3] explain this mindset saying that in a pietistic church, our actions are used to determine our identity as a Christian rather than our identity as a Christian determining our actions. It's a very subtle, nuanced difference, but an important one. In practice, it sounds like, "If you talk back to your parents, you may not be a Christian" versus "As a Christian, over time the Holy Spirit will help you desire to respect your parents."

Our pietistic church instilled a micro-focus on the actions and mindset of believers as we slogged along in our continual, unrelenting pursuit of Christ-like perfection. We worried about whether we were trying hard enough as we cultivated an external appearance of righteousness without regard to Matthew 23:27 which reads, "Woe unto you, scribes and Pharisees, hypocrites! for ye are like unto whited sepulchers, which indeed appear beautiful outward, but are within full of dead men's bones, and of all uncleanness."

I heard that verse preached once in the fundamentalist church, but the punchline was to double down on our personal improvement projects. It was a self-righteous focus on the ongoing works of the believer rather than the completed work of Jesus. Whited sepulchers don't know they are whited sepulchers. They are too busy focusing on their own works and judging others who display any visible flaws in the whitewash.

For example, when the pastor preached on the second half of Jesus' Sermon on the Mount teachings found in Matthew 5, he warned that the standard we were all expected to meet was high. After all this passage includes excerpts like, "whosoever looketh on a woman to lust after her hath committed adultery with her already in his heart" and "whosoever is angry with his brother without a cause shall be in danger of the judgment."

As I remember it, although the audience was a room full of believers, we were essentially told based on this passage we were still abject failures who were living in perpetual danger of incurring God's wrathful judgment if we didn't live up to this lofty standard.

Matthew 5 concludes with verse 48 which states, "Be ye therefore perfect, even as your Father which is in heaven is perfect."

Imagine how this verse may be applied in a fundamentalist church that focuses on following existing laws and further legislating believers into obedience while promoting the self-policing mindset of continual evaluation of our efforts. In such context, rather than dramatically highlighting the clear need for Jesus based on the understood impossibility of human perfection, verse 48 can quite literally be understood as instructing Christians that we must be as perfect as God. Full stop.

That's certainly how I came to understand the verse. God expected perfection from me, not so I would earn salvation as other religious sects believed, but so I would prove I had already received it. If I couldn't prove my salvation through my perfect ability to live out the law, then perhaps I was not really saved.

I was about fourteen or fifteen years old at the time and not yet free to walk out or make any response to these judgements and teachings. Since it wasn't an emotionally or socially safe place to ask questions, my options were limited. I simply had to sit and take it, then go home where the message percolated in my psyche for the rest of the day, its word shards jabbing at my already tender pietistical conscience.

Often, I dutifully followed along and took notes on the sermon. Other times, I would try to escape mentally by imagining I was somewhere else. I later learned this is called disassociation.

I would absorb myself in daydreams of beautiful places where love and sparkling joy surrounded me. I imagined soaring through the sky with the northern lights, walking along glowing bioluminescent beaches at night, or exploring space with all its nebulas and galaxies.

On other days, I would simply doodle and draw on the bulletin. I sketched out my bedroom and the furniture—dreaming up ways to rearrange it and refresh the space. Some weeks I would follow through and physically move the furniture when I got home from church. Though I did not consciously realize it at the time, this action gave me a semblance of control and a sense of ability to shape my own reality in a world where so much was dictated by others.

Still, the day would leave me with a bitter taste, heavy guilt, and a cloud of depression that lingered through the night. I looked forward to school washing it away the next day. Even with the inevitable bullying, it was still better than being trapped in church.

No Need for a Physician

The context I was being given and the inferences I was silently drawing during these Sunday morning sermons influenced my understanding of other verses and passages as well. One of the most important of these was Matthew 9:11-13: "And when the Pharisees saw it, they said unto his disciples, Why eateth your Master with publicans and sinners? But when Jesus heard that, he said unto them, They that be whole need not a physician, but they that are sick. But go ye and learn what that meaneth, I will have mercy, and not sacrifice: for I am not come to call the righteous, but sinners to repentance." The book of Mark covers this moment as well in Mark 2:17.

By the time I was ten years old, I had internalized the pietistic mentality to such an extent it felt natural. Within this paradigm, I understood the passage from Matthew to mean the Pharisees were doing their part and living up to the law. Jesus was simply telling them he needed to go take care of all the slackers that weren't strong enough and couldn't cut it on their own.

My takeaway was that I was supposed to step it up and be one of the self-sufficient "whole" because Jesus had enough to do with all those other "sick" people who needed a physician. Don't be the squeaky wheel who causes problems by needing a physician.

I applied the same reasoning to the story about Jesus leaving the ninety-nine sheep to find the one that has gone astray. You really didn't want to be that one sheep who he had to go looking for because you got out of line and weren't doing what you were supposed to be doing.

A Woman's Place

Fundamental churches typically believe in complementary roles for males and females. Legalistic fundamentalists take this a step further with extremely specific prescribed visions of all aspects of appropriate conduct and deportment.

As girls, the template for living a good fundamentalist Christian life looked something like this:

We were to start out as toddlers simply sitting quietly during church and not kicking the pew in front of us or trying to rip pages out of the hymnal. Fair enough. Next, we moved on to memorizing Bible verses and the lyrics to children's church songs. We were taught to respect and honor our parents, not talk back, clean our rooms, and be agreeable and social to peers and adults. Again, pretty standard.

We would ask Jesus to be our savior—probably as young children and certainly before adolescence. When we were still pre-teens, most of us would be baptized publicly in front of our congregation as a testimony to our faith. During this time, we would witness to our peers and bring them into the fold as well where, as young legalists in training, they too would learn the rules of our religion and how to check all the boxes of the law so God would be pleased.

When we became teens, we would treat our bodies as temples—no smoking, drinking, tattoos, or piercings (except maybe a single ear piercing for women, though even that may be frowned upon). We would remain pure, we would save ourselves for marriage, and as females, we would of course avoid wearing any sort of clothing that could "cause our brother to stumble."

We would attend church and Sunday school each week, volunteer in the nursery during services, and take part in the youth group program until we were old enough to become youth group leaders to the next generation of children.

We would not be depressed, anxious, stressed, or filled with anything other than a bright and shining hope for our futures because, "If Christ be for us, who can be against us?" We would wait for God to show us our path in life and call us to whatever ministry he had in store.

When we met an Independent Fundamental Baptist male we found attractive and our family and church approved of, we would studiously avoid physical touch beyond perhaps holding hands because it was a slippery slope, and the devil was waiting at the bottom like Jaws, ready to devour us.

Our suitor would respectfully court us and ask our father's permission to marry us. Following the wedding, we would move into our new two-bedroom, one-bath house and likely very shortly afterward become pregnant with our first child because birth control was generally frowned upon. Together we would take our offspring to church and began anew the cycle of training up a child in the fundamentalist way.

As women in the church, we may work outside the home, not because that should be the way of things but simply because it was recognized that in this "fallen world," it was all but a financial necessity for most families.

We would keep the house clean, have dinner on the table, and ensure all our husband's and children's needs were met. We would have time to cook food for the church potluck (or pot 'blessing' if your pietistic spirit is uncomfortable with the word 'luck'). We would bake cookies for the bake sale and keep ourselves physically, emotionally, mentally, and spiritually attractive to our husband and to God.

Our husband was ordained to be the head of the household, and as such, we would submit to his authority in all things, second only to God. We would exemplify all the virtues of biblical womanhood per Proverbs 31, and each week we would sit through sermons from the man in the pulpit who would be fond of telling us how we failed to measure up.

• • •

I learned a lot about the power of words through sermons on topics like submission. In junior high, when the preacher was talking about how women (and we girls as future women) were to submit to their husbands, just that word generated so many emotions in me.

To be fair, the Bible *does* tell women to "submit" to their husbands, but the tone in which pastors often instruct good fundamentalist Christian girls and women to do so sounds more akin to "subjugate."

When I heard these types of sermons, I felt anger that I was not being considered an equal. I felt fear that my future husband would be allowed to walk all over me, and the church would support it. I felt a deep existential hurt that had no name.

Why was I seemingly being told I was less than, that this was the natural order of things, and that my place as a woman someday would be to support my husband and his dreams, not to pursue mine as an equal partner in the relationship?

This idea of a woman's place in the fundamentalist world was reinforced for me in high school through something as simple and personal as my choice of haircut.

I really enjoy having long, flowy hair and have only cut my hair short a couple times (not counting the ill-advised DIY bang trimming debacle which immediately preceded my kindergarten Christmas concert).

As I started my sophomore year of high school, I wanted a change. I had been reading about Locks of Love, and I thought if I were going to cut my hair anyway, it may as well be a nice long length that could be made into a wig for a cancer patient. My hairdresser and I decided to cut off twelve inches, turning my mid-back length mane into a just above the shoulders bob.

After my hair cut, I stopped by the parsonage to visit my friend, the pastor's daughter. When I arrived, her dad walked out to greet me. He looked me up and down then rebuked me. "Remember, a woman's hair is her covering." That was in reference to 1 Corinthians 11:15: "But if a woman have long hair, it is a glory to her: for her hair is given her for a covering."

Verse 5 of this same chapter is used by some other very conservative fundamentalist religious sects to advocate that woman wear some form of hair covering as well (better to be doubly covered than not at all, I suppose). "But every woman that prayeth or prophesieth with her head uncovered dishonoureth her head: for that is even all one as if she were shaven" (1 Corinthians 11:5).

In my case, the religion of my childhood counted my hair as a covering and decided to forego the bonnets and hats. Still, this interaction with our pastor and his rebuking me over theological minutia was another reminder of my place as a woman in a fundamentalist church and of all the legalistic strings, expectations, and dogma that came along with accepting the "free gift of salvation."

All this is a taste of the crippling and unattainable path I saw laid out for a fundamentalist Christian woman to walk. Unattainable, yet I was raised to believe if I were a true Christian who was following Jesus and living a godly life, all things would be possible through Christ, who strengthened me, so I tried—goodness knows I tried. I tried so hard.

True Love Waits

For a fundamentalist girl, virginity is considered your utmost virtue. Your purity is the gift you must guard until you present it to your husband on your wedding night. Your husband will hopefully be a virgin too, but if he is not, that is okay. He is, after all, only human, and God will forgive him.

I came of age in the late-90s and early-2000s in a fundamental culture infatuated with the purity movement. The ideals of the *True Love Waits* campaign[4] and Joshua Harris' *I Kissed Dating Goodbye*[5] book heavily informed many conservative churches' viewpoints on teenage relationships during this time.

Dating was a serious business for fundamentalists. After all, dating is meant to be courting, and courting is focused on marital compatibility. That is a lot to put on a sixteen-year-old who is still figuring out how to drive a car and who often neglects to put gas in the gas tank before the said car is running on fumes.

Some girls were forbidden to date at all, though my parents opted for the slightly more liberal choice of allowing dating once my sister and I reached the age of sixteen. I still had my first awkward middle school kiss on our school gymnasium's balcony when I was fourteen, but my actual first date was reserved for after my sixteenth birthday.

For a girl who has before God committed to staying sexually pure until marriage, every encounter with a member of the opposite sex is laced with a certain degree of concern and fear. We were told repeatedly what a slippery slope we were on with all our raging teenage hormones.

Making eye contact leads to holding hands, which leads to kissing, which leads to touching, then to groping, and ultimately to sin. Our bodies were temples to be kept pure and holy for God. We were to resist the temptations of the flesh.

The tradeoff for our faithfulness, or so we were told, was an all but guaranteed mind-blowingly amazing sexual relationship with our future husbands. If we remained sweet and innocent virgins now, on our wedding night, we believed we would be miraculously transformed into a seductive vixen of a woman with all the sexual prowess and skills to rock our new husbands' worlds.

Girls who wanted to acknowledge their continued virginal status in a cheeky way would wear shirts printed with sayings like, "Saving myself for wild wedding night sex." We somehow believed that despite the total inexperience and ineptitude of both ourselves and our husbands, we would instantaneously have the perfect sexual experience God had created us to enjoy within the bounds of matrimony.

Unequally Yoked

Many conservative churches refuse to marry a believer and an unbeliever knowingly, citing 2 Corinthians 6:14: "Be ye not unequally yoked together with unbelievers: for what fellowship hath righteousness with unrighteousness? and what communion hath light with darkness?"

When I started dating the man who would eventually become my first husband, Rob, I was sixteen. He was nineteen. I was a believer. He was not, and the weight of that verse laid heavy with guilt upon me.

Did dating count as being yoked? Was I sinning simply by dating him? What if I could convince him to become a believer? Would that subsequent conversion negate the initial sin of unequal yoking, like a retroactive offset? These are the convoluted conversations I had with myself as I tried to work through the problem.

On several late-night calls, I remember hounding him about the status of his soul. I am ashamed to say I badgered him and badgered him out of my own fear and guilt. It was never so much about what might happen to him after death, as it was about how much trouble I would be in if he did not convert.

Finally, after a few months, I gave him an ultimatum: if he did not become a believer, I would have to break up with him. I was filled with pompous, righteous piety. He was filled with infatuation and love.

A day later, he told me he had accepted Jesus as his savior. He joined our church (we had just left the fundamentalist

Baptist church and had moved to a non-denominational Bible church). That summer, Rob was baptized. Everyone was so moved by his bold confession of faith. I was relieved to have dodged the guilt bullet.

By that time, the layers of fundamentalist doctrine had built on top of one another until, I could barely keep up with it all.

Treading the waters of legalism in search of the unattainable perfection that was supposed to supply peace had become exhausting. I was drowning in dogma and an overwhelming sense of insurmountable failure.

Reflection Invite: Part 1

1. My spiritual beliefs have been shaped and molded by

_____

_____

_____

_____

_____

_____

_____.

2. A defining moment in my spiritual life and development was when _____.

_____

_____

_____

_____

_____.

This moment was important because

_____

_____

_____

_____

_____.

3. Based on how I was raised, I believed God was _____

_____

_____

_____

_____

_____

_____.

4. My faith community expected me to _____

_____

_____

_____

_____.

If I were unable or unwilling to meet those expectations

_____

_____

_____

_____

_____.

When that happened, I felt _____

_____

_____ and responded by

_____

_____.

PART 2
LEAVING FUNDAMENTALISM

Courage doesn't happen when you have all the answers. It happens when you are ready to face the questions you have been avoiding your whole life.

—Shannon L. Alder

CHAPTER 4

QUESTIONS WITHOUT ANSWERS

Having been raised in the fundamentalist atmosphere that I was, for the first fourteen or fifteen years of my life, I accepted everything I was taught within our church as the 100% full and exact truth.

Any problems I had living up to the standards that were set, I chalked up to my own shameful inadequacies that somehow other church members appeared to be impervious to. The confusing and unanswered scriptural questions I had were signs of my own limited understanding, not a potential flaw in the teaching or explanation of the pastor.

The need to understand the truth is clear from an early age. Ask the parents of any three-year-old, and they will tell you their kid's favorite question is some variation of "Why?" We are born to ask questions and seek truth.

I wanted to know the truth, but my church did not invite questioning. Instead, I had been taught church leadership would share whatever truths we needed to know.

Asking tough questions meant your faith as a believer was weak.

If you were not fully committed, on fire, and 100% on board with everything the church said, you might find yourself viewed with concern the way people eye a stray dog who they think could snarl, lunge, bite, and infect them with rabies at any second. You were at risk of becoming one of those dreaded "backsliders" or "lukewarm Christians." No one wanted to be associated with such a person because, after all, God hated lukewarm Christians and was known to have spat them out of his mouth.

The idea of being spit out never made sense to me since it seemingly flew in the face of the "once saved, always saved" doctrine my church preached. The only thing I could come up with was that perhaps if you were a lukewarm Christian and were spit out, it did not mean God threw you in the trash, but rather that he put you back in the pot on the stove and heated you up again until you reached a temperature more pleasing to his palate.

Of course, this sounded rather painful and reminded me of lobsters being boiled alive, so I was not entirely sure it would be better than having been spat into the trash.

The bottom line was that at this point, I genuinely wanted to understand, but was confused and it didn't feel safe to ask any of my unspoken questions.

Violence in the Bible

For example, as I read the Bible, certain verses and stories stuck out as jarringly harsh, distasteful, or even unconscionable to me. I noticed many sermons glossed over the details of these narratives or avoided them altogether, though some touted the harsh retributions as clearly justified. The more

I listened and read, the more I noticed a list of confusing and scary horrors.

For example, in 2 Samuel and 1 Chronicles, when Uzzah touched the Ark of the Covenant to stabilize it as it was in danger of falling while being carried across the desert, he was killed. Why? The oxen slipped, the Ark shifted, and Uzzah reached out to keep it from falling. By all accounts, he was merely trying to keep this sacred vessel safe. I did not understand why that act seemingly merited a death sentence.

In multiple conquest stories, God commanded the Israelites to kill all the men and children but to keep the virgin women for themselves. In Hosea 13:16, God ordered the infants of the Samarians be "dashed in pieces," and pregnant women be "ripped up" because of the people's rebellion.

What kind of higher morality did it demonstrate to kill the infants, unborn children, and the women carrying them? Why would God condone the rape of women and treating women as property? Yes, that may have been a human norm at the time, but shouldn't God's morals be higher than human morals and God's ways more advanced and enlightened than man's? Why were the children and infants allowed to become collateral damage for their parents' misdeeds? I had no answers.

Speaking of killings, I knew the numbers were high. I later learned that when Steve Wells, author of the *Skeptic's Annotated Bible*[6], added up the totals for all the killings that God either conducted himself, ordered, or approved of, the body count was a stunning 2,821,364. This number reflects only the deaths we are given totals for. When he made his best estimates to include the rest of the sanctioned killings the Bible does not supply data for, Wells arrived at a total of roughly twenty-five million. That is a lot of death and destruction in the name of God.

Then there is childhood trauma. Can you imagine how poor Isaac felt after Abraham led him up Mount Sinai to offer a sacrifice, and then Isaac found out *he* was meant to be the sacrifice? Yes, he was spared in the end and the whole scene was an allegory for God supplying Jesus as the perfect lamb, but how did that impact the relationship between Isaac and Abraham? How was Isaac able to trust his father or God after that? Could he ever again feel safe?

On the rare occasions I heard anyone else tentatively express these types of concerns, they were often handed cliché responses like, "God works in mysterious ways," or "Who are we to understand the will of God?" We could ask him when we got to Heaven, but for now, we just needed to have faith.

Sometimes the answer was that those situations happened in the Old Testament under the old covenant and that with the New Testament and the new covenant through Jesus, things were different. Well, I thought, tell that to Ananias and Sapphira, who were killed for lying and saying they had given the church all the proceeds from the sale of their home and property. Was it right to lie about it so they could look noble in the eyes of the church? No. Did that deserve instantaneous death? Apparently, God thought so.

The Purpose of Prayer

Even prayer became confusing for me. On the one hand, we were told prayer was a way for us to communicate with God. It was us talking directly to our Heavenly Father. On the other hand, I noticed many prayers I heard seemed formulaic. They felt and sounded more like someone reading a script than engaging in heartfelt conversation. If the Lord's Prayer was meant to be an example—a template—of how to pray, why did so many believers keep regurgitating the template instead of personalizing it and using it as a guide and an example of the genuine communication that prayer was designed to be?

Another thing that troubled me was the concept of public prayer. The only measurable difference I could see between public prayer and speeches was that speeches were delivered with your eyes open. Other than that, the two types of public speaking seemed indistinguishable.

From what I saw, both public speaking and public prayer required the speaker to prepare what they were going to say in advance. Both were delivered in a specific oratory fashion designed in such a way as to get the listener to follow along and buy into what was being said. Both felt calculated. They were designed to make the speaker look and sound good—to elevate his or her status in the eyes of the audience.

That was fine in the case of a public speech, but what about public prayer? In that context, it reminded me of the New Testament stories of the Pharisees and Sadducees of Jesus' time, showing off their superior levels of knowledge and righteousness without the raw genuineness and openness I equated with an actual conversation.

One of the most damaging examples of prayer I was given was that of parents using prayer as a weapon.

I remember hearing a mother pray aloud in front of her children that they would be better behaved tomorrow than they had been today. As she went on telling God how disobedient and disrespectful her children had been, I wondered what purpose she would have to do so in front of them in such an aggressive way rather than saving it for a private moment simply between her and God. Her prayer seemed less meant to ask for God's intercession than it was an untouchable pedestal from which to chastise her children.

A Conditional Love

We learn how to love through the examples of our closest and earliest role models. The love they show to us and in front of us is what we naturally carry forward into all our future relationships.

At the beginning of my life, I was loved in the most beautiful way by my parents, my grandparents, and the people around me. I felt safe, loved, and worthy. I gave and received love freely, willingly, and effortlessly.

Then the expectations showed up, the caveats and the conditions. The message I internalized was, yes, you are loved, but you are loved if you meet certain criteria.

You are lovable if you are submissive. You are lovable if you are obedient. You are lovable if you comply with what your parents and your church tell you to do and believe. You are lovable if you are perfect.

That is love.

To be fair, there were also some sermons describing philia or agape love and reminding us to love our neighbors as ourselves, but I did not feel and experience much of that love in practice.

The "Christian love" I experienced in the fundamentalist faith was a harsh love, a judging love, a pietistic love obsessed with keeping track of one's transgressions and failures. It was a transactional love given in exchange for dutifully following the program and externally living up to the standards and rules set forth by church leadership.

Such a love must be earned, and by the time I was fifteen, I wasn't so sure I could keep earning it much longer.

Perhaps you have experienced this form of love as well either from a faith community or from family. It is a damaging love with the power to echo well into adulthood.

I am lovable if I predict all my partner's needs. I am lovable if I say yes to any request anyone makes of me regardless of how overtasked I already am. I am lovable if I take on extra work to bring in more money. I am lovable if I bake homemade cookies for my kid's elementary school bake sale rather than buying a box from the store. I am lovable if I lose that extra ten pounds. I am lovable if...

...I am lovable *if.*

CHAPTER 5
THROUGH THE VALLEY

During my childhood, someone gave me a bookmark with the image of a beautiful sandy beach. On it was printed one of the most famous Christian poems: *Footprints*. It is about someone dreaming and looking back on the path of life as they walk along the sandy beach with God beside them.

In the sand are two sets of footprints, except for during the hardest, saddest moments. In those moments, one set of footprints disappears. This concerns the dreamer, who asks why God would simply vanish and abandon him during the rough patches. God's response?

"When you saw only one set of footprints, it was then that I carried you."

I never knew what to make of that. On the one hand, it was comforting to think if life got to be too much and I just could not manage it, there was a way to wave the white flag and be scooped up and taken care of. On the other hand, how did that align with the teaching about God never giving us more than we could handle?

I wondered if this *Footprints* God was legitimate or fabricated. He sounded too loving to be real. He certainly did not sound like the "God of Wrath" I heard preached from my church's pulpit. Still, the image of curling up, nestled like a child safe against the chest of a loving, caring, protective God seemed so warm and inviting. I wanted that. I craved that, especially after my grandpa died, and the feelings of depression intensified. I longed for a "personal Jesus," one who would scoop me up in his arms, draw me close, and hold me with the most intensely beautiful, all-enveloping love.

I prayed for this personal Jesus. As the questions about my childhood faith started mounting, I asked more fervently that if God and Jesus were indeed real, would they please come to be with me, hold me, care for me, love me, and protect me in that way.

I asked and waited, but I felt nothing. I experienced nothing—just a vast, frigid, empty void.

My beach was rocky and cold, with powerful waves crashing on the shores every moment, threatening to wash me away into the unforgiving sea. I left no footprints on that harsh wasteland, but if I had, I was quite sure there would only be one set, and my bloody knees were testament to the fact that no one had been carrying *me* when the wave of my grandpa's death hit and slammed me into the jagged boulders of grief.

Only Believers Go to Heaven

You hear a lot about people questioning or walking away from their faith when a loved one dies. They ask, "How could this happen?" and "Why does God allow pain and suffering?" They want to know why God did not prevent the pain of the loss or, depending on their beliefs, why he caused it in the first place.

When Granpa died, I was fifteen, and I did not have those questions. In that moment, I had no questions at all, really. What I had was anger and disgust.

I heard my parents talking about how my mom did not think her mom and dad were true believers. They went to church on Christmas Eve and maybe Easter, but to the best of Mom's knowledge, her parents had not actually asked Jesus to be their savior. Mom told Dad it made her sad her parents were not going to Heaven when they died.

I remember sitting in the backseat of the car during this exchange and picturing my wonderfully loving and selflessly generous grandpa and grandma—two people who had shown me true unconditional love in my life. I considered what my mother had just said, and I felt utter disgust, anger, and hatred toward the idea of a deity that would be so petty as to send my grandparents to a pit of eternally burning fire simply for not having confirmed his existence.

Was it not enough that God had to take my freedom, my happiness, my self-esteem, my peace, my joy, and my ability to love and be loved in a healthy way? Now he was also laying claim to two people who had genuinely loved me and showed me they loved me in a no-strings-attached manner? And I was supposed to shut up and follow him anyway? Absolutely not! If that was what love was, and what Gramma and Granpa had done deserved Hell, well then, I wanted nothing to do with Heaven.

After Granpa's funeral was over, we went back to our house, where my mom, aunts, and cousins played games and laughed over slices of pizza. I did not join in. It made no sense to me how a person could laugh and seemingly enjoy life when they believed someone they loved was in a place of never-ending torture.

It Is Your Fault

How do you respond when someone you care about opens up to you and shares they have been struggling with depression or anxiety? When they reveal their life does not seem to be getting better no matter what they do, what do you say?

As a legalistic pietist, you might launch into a series of questions about their church attendance, how often they have been doing their devotionals and praying, or even what sort of hidden sin they might have in their life.

You would ask these things because you have been taught that to feel depression or anxiety, to struggle with any sort of mental illness or mood disorder is a certain indicator of a self-induced disconnect from God, the great physician. If someone is feeling mentally or emotionally unwell, it must be their fault. They are doing something wrong in their walk with God.

I heard of this message being given to other women who were brave (or misguided) enough to come forward to church leaders and voice their struggle. I did not remember hearing any questions or talk about whether they had gone to their doctor to get their hormone and vitamin levels checked. I heard nothing about what they were eating, how they were sleeping, or if perhaps they had a baby recently and could be going through postpartum depression or anxiety. There were no questions about any sort of emotional or social situations that could contribute to their condition. The response was simply one of asking them about their walk with God—as though their actions there were the sole cause of or remedy for any malaise.

Although I did not personally witness it, some pietists applied the same line of reasoning to physical ailments like cancer. In those intensely pietistic circles, serious illness can be viewed as a way of God getting your attention since you rebelliously refused to listen to his earlier gentler nudging to change your life.

If you have cancer, it is your own fault for not being a good enough Christian and obeying properly so Jesus would protect you. What kind of a message is that?

I heard those stories and learned that if I were ever in a similar position, I better keep my mouth shut and my Noh mask on.

Looking back on it now, searching for any charitable explanation, the best I can muster is that perhaps those pastors and elders were merely intending to gauge their parishioner's spiritual health while assuming a doctor would assess the physical, and a therapist would check the psychological and emotional. Perhaps the pastors' sole focus was on the spiritual because that was their area of expertise not because they were purposely dismissing all the rest.

The problem was, by pursuing a line of accusatory questioning when a woman came to them with a need, the pastor risked beating down an already hurting soul and making her feel guilty for causing her own condition. That guilt could make a woman less likely to seek any sort of treatment or tools and more likely to internalize and try to mask the pain until she simply could not anymore because she thought that was what God expected of her.

I know because I became one of those women.

That's Not It, Is It?

In the year-and-a-half following my grandpa's death, the feelings of depression, powerlessness, and hopelessness

grew. While seeking a feeling—any feeling—through causing myself physical pain, I also tried calorie restriction for
a brief time. It was one of the few areas of my life over
which I seemed to have any control. My parents and church
determined my reality on this planet, and God held my
afterlife—an afterlife where I would apparently not see my
grandpa. At least I could control the food I put into my body.

After long days at school, I would come home and
immediately get online to spend as much of the evening
as possible chatting on AOL Instant Messenger with my
best friend, Beth. She understood where I was coming
from—she grew up in a conservative, fundamental sect of
the Lutheran church. Still, her Lutheran God was much
more loving than my fundamentalist Baptist God.

We discussed that difference at length, and it both-
ered us both that we could, in theory, believe in the same
God, but our reality of the relationship with him could
be so radically different. Her God was there to help her,
guide her, and look out for her. My God felt like he was
there to manipulate my life as though I were a pawn in a
cosmic pre-ordained chess game. My God was controlling,
micromanaging, and harsh—a perpetual "God of Wrath"
who was "quick to anger."

After over a year of living this way and trying to make
sense of the pain, depression, hollowness, and dull ache, I
was in tenth grade—still an awfully long, two-plus years
from moving away to college. That carrot seemed impos-
sibly and unattainably distant. I doubted my ability to
make it so far, the way things were.

When we chatted just before Christmas break was to
start, I told Beth I simply could not do it anymore. I said I
was going to end it and commit suicide on Christmas Eve.

The day had always been so special and beautiful to
me. We would get dressed up and go over to Gramma and

Granpa's house for dinner. As we drove up the driveway, we were greeted by the red wreaths and illuminated candles in the windows. Inside, the delicious aromas of a lovingly prepared dinner wafted through the house.

After we ate, we were tempted to tear into the presents waiting in the living room, but first, we all bundled up and went off to the Lutheran church my grandparents attended this one night a year.

The lighting in the sanctuary was soft and warm; the decorated tree sparkled with ornaments and garlands. We were each handed a little white candle that slid through the hole of a ruby red cup designed to catch the drips of molten wax.

As the service ended, the lights dimmed even further. We lit our candles, and together we sang a beautiful acapella rendition of "Silent Night" before snuggling into our coats and heading back to Gramma and Granpa's house for the much-anticipated gift opening.

When we finally got home, usually shortly before midnight, Karen and I quickly put out a glass of milk, a plate of Finnish prune tart and thumbprint cookies we had baked ourselves, plus several carrots for the reindeer. My mom recited Clement Moore's poem, *The Night Before Christmas*, for us, we read the story of Jesus' birth from the Book of Luke, and we hurried to bed before Santa arrived.

This Christmas Eve routine was beautiful, precious, and, in my mind, timeless—until my grandpa's death.

Now, a year-and-a-half later, as Christmas Eve approached, I felt like I could not do it anymore. I could not keep slogging through, could not keep putting on the mask and acting the part.

And I certainly could not navigate another formerly joyous night and sing about sleeping in heavenly peace when I was told Granpa was most certainly not experiencing that peace, and there was nothing I could do about it.

So, I told Beth that Christmas Eve was the night.

In the eighteen months since my grandpa had died, I had dragged Beth with me through the muddy waters of my quietly hidden grief and the soul-searing iciness of deepening depression.

The fact that she is still my closest friend today is a testament to the depth of her love and compassion for me because it would have been one-hundred percent fair for her to have run.

How many of us as grown adults feel equipped to be with someone we love and walk them through that dark place? It was far too much to ask of any sixteen-year-old, yet for a year-and-a-half, she did it and did it the best she knew how. She loved me when I was unlovable, forgave me when I was unforgivable, and offered me all the understanding, support, and warmth that could still never hope to fill the void or heal the pain.

Finally, when I inked an end date to all the darkness, she knew it was a secret she no longer could or should keep, so filled with fear of my response, she handed it off to the one adult we both trusted more than anyone—our band director, Mr. Boyd.

Beth and Brit, a mutual friend of ours, went over to Mr. B's house to tell him, and then the three of them called me on my cell phone that night as I was curled up in my bed.

Mr. Boyd lived only a short drive from my house, and he asked me to come over so we could all talk in person. I said no, out of fear of how I would explain the anomaly to my parents. I somehow still thought they were not going to find out what was going on, even though an adult was now involved.

I promised Beth, Brit, and Mr. Boyd I wasn't going to off myself that night and would just go back to bed. As I hung up the phone, I thought that was it; the next day would be back to business as usual.

It was too—until the guidance counselor came down and interrupted my civics class to say they needed to see me in his office. With a sinking feeling and racing heart, I followed him upstairs.

My parents were seated in a conference room, my dad still in his mechanic's work clothes, and my mother with makeup applied so quickly she had forgotten to blend in the foundation under her nose.

I avoided the awkward eye contact the best I could and slid into the designated chair at the far end of the table. The years have since blurred out exactly what the counselor said, but he must have asked something about whether I was mad at Beth and Brit for telling Mr. B.

When I said no, they opened the door and ushered both girls in. As soon as I saw them, an intense wave of deep, piercing betrayal flooded through me.

My face must have displayed the harsh emotion clearly because the girls turned and left the room as quickly as they had entered.

After the meeting, my dad went back to work while my mom was tasked with taking me directly from school to an urgent doctor's appointment for a clinical evaluation.

I refused to talk with the doctor while my mom was in the room, and the next thing I knew, it was just the doctor and me.

She asked me something like why I was feeling the way I was and what had motivated me to consider suicide as a solution.

Surprising myself, I candidly shared the truth that church was at the root of it.

She was clearly taken aback, and, as a believer herself, she seemed instinctively uncomfortable, incredulous, and reflexively dismissive of the idea that the church could be in any way culpable for what I was experiencing.

"That's not it, is it?"

In one crisp, devastating sentence, she verbally brushed aside and negated the delicate truth I had so tenuously managed to offer up while at the same time clearly communicating to me that I had best agree with her to preserve her comfort and not venture into the dangerous grounds of being sacrilegious.

"No," I softly acquiesced, bottling the truth back up and raising my Noh mask.

My truth, I realized, was not welcome here. I would not speak it again until I reached the safety of adulthood.

CHAPTER 6
BROKEN PROMISES

I was an eighteen-year-old college freshman when my high school sweetheart, Rob, asked me to marry him. I had broken up with Rob during the summer before leaving home for a college five hundred miles away (as far away from my hometown as possible while still qualifying for in-state tuition rates).

Though I loved him, a part of me had wanted to experience more and live more before committing to such an irrevocable decision as marriage. When we broke up, my mother was devastated. She viewed him as the son she never had, and they had developed a close relationship which they maintain to this day.

The shared reflection of his and her pain was too great and brought too much guilt to bear, so after only a couple of days, I asked Rob to come over to our house. He walked in the door, and I immediately brought him over to my mother. I presented him to her as you would a gift, saying simply, "I have something for you." She lit up, as did he, and at that moment, I knew Rob and I would end up together. I could not break both their hearts a second time.

Rob asked me to marry him over a perfect dinner with a beautiful marquise diamond ring that shimmered exactly as I imagined it would when I pictured the moment as a little girl. Like any man who understood traditional conservative culture, Rob had asked my father's permission to propose to me and had received his blessing.

When I imagined the moment of my proposal, I always expected to be filled with pure excitement and to respond with a resounding "yes" without a shred of doubt or uncertainty in me. "Of *course*, this is the man I want to spend the rest of my life with. Of *course,* this is the father of my future children. Of *course,* I will love and grow old with this man. Yes!"

I did say "yes." The moment I accepted his proposal, I shoved the spark of fear and the thready whispers of doubt deep down inside, choosing instead to focus on the excitement of the pretty ring, dress shopping, and planning a perfect wedding.

After all, I loved him, and he loved me. What reason was there to wait? He had jumped through all the hoops of joining my faith, getting baptized, supporting me through depression. My family loved him, and we seemed destined to be together. We were good friends.

Besides, we had been dating for over two years. In that time, my sexual purity had already been tarnished by our illicit kissing, spooning, and touching. The technicality of my virginity was all I had left, so a little voice said, *you better hurry up and get married before you* **really** *sin by completely crossing that line*—so much guilt.

Shortly after our engagement, when my mom carefully asked if I was sure about the marriage, I brushed off the question, too terrified of opening that Pandora's box. Later, I confided in Beth that I felt like I simply had no choice and could not say no even if I tried. I was destined to marry him.

Looking back, I wonder how many other young Christians get married early for some of these same reasons—wanting not to sin and trying to do the right thing any way they can. Not all will have the strength to wait for the right marriage to the right spouse at the right time, as my sister did.

It is easy to say wait, but the support systems are not always in place. When the waiting gets hard or long, and we are not prepared for it, some of us will rush into a commitment we are not yet ready for.

When Christians marry young, some of those marriages do prosper. Others of us either spend our whole lives settling for and navigating a less than ideal relationship or we divorce.

The Wedding Night

If all those years of preserving my purity and protecting my virginity were the buildup, the payoff was promised to be on my wedding night. I would say my vows at one in the afternoon as a pristine and innocent bride.

Twelve hours later, after the photos, the cake, and the dancing, my new husband and I would arrive in our bridal suite. There I believed I would instantaneously be imbued with everything I needed to know so we would have an incredible steamy night of marital sex.

I had never seen a naked man. My baseline knowledge for what to do with one was limited to what I had read in an old paperback copy of *Everything You Always Wanted to Know About Sex...But Were Too Afraid to Ask*.

This reference, a sort of "how-to and here's how it can go wrong" manual, was supplemented by bits of illicit information gleaned from the pages of *Cosmopolitan* and the passing descriptions of sex in some of my favorite books which tended to approach it from a "the woman's role is to provide the man pleasure" standpoint.

Although Rob and I attended pre-marital counseling through the church, I remember the conversations being largely about other important aspects like finances, daily life, and conflict resolution. These topics certainly had value, but the discussions and readings did little to prepare us for our wedding night physically, mentally, emotionally, or spiritually.

I can now most charitably describe that night as two kindergarteners trying to teach each other how to write. My final memory of our wedding night is of rolling over in the king-size bed of our lovely Victorian bridal suite, trying to hide the tears of confusion from my poor new husband, who I hoped had at least somehow managed to enjoy the highly anticipated experience.

Wifely Duties

The next day we tried again, and that time at least, the mechanics of the act were physically possible if not remotely enjoyable for me. I remember unabashedly calling my mom and proudly announcing, "I had sex with my husband!"

Her upbeat enthusiasm helped to assuage the rapidly building sea of fear and despair that was welling up inside me.

Was that all there was? Had I waited so long only for this horridly wretched experience? How many more times in my life would I have to carry out this "wifely duty?" The years of obligatory sex stretched out in front of me in a bleak row further than I could see.

During our European honeymoon, I only remember us having sex once in a small hotel room in downtown London. He seemed to enjoy it, and while the depression and revulsion I felt at the act were building, I noted my ability to hide it was also improving.

After all, providing my husband with physical gratification was something God expected of me. I was a good Christian wife, pleasing her husband. I had made my bed, and now it was time to sleep in it, literally.

The anger did not develop right away. It was preceded by an emotion I was far more familiar with—guilt. In line with the true pietistic mentality in which I was raised, I viewed my difficulties with and distaste of sex as obviously indicative of my own personal failings and incompetence.

Here is the two-fold problem as I now see it: First, I had been raised to view premarital sex as a critical sin of the highest order, and one that would doom my future marriage to failure. So much value had been placed on my virginity, but I did not realize how much of my self-worth was wrapped up in my status as a virginal woman until it was time to relinquish said virginity.

Waking up the morning after my wedding, I felt dirty. I felt defiled. I felt like a piece of me—the one I had been told for so long was the key to my worth as a Christian woman—was gone. I had clumsily given that gift to my husband as promised, but who was I now?

The second problem was I had walked down that aisle holding the belief that sexual compatibility and chemistry were a given—that our sacrifices and abstinence leading up to this incredibly special day would be rewarded with marital fireworks and complete bliss.

We had saved ourselves for marriage, and for what? Where was the fulfillment of that promise? Where was the fairytale ending? Anger started to build within me as I felt lied to and cheated.

• • •

It was not until years later that I learned the psychology and physiology behind what had happened to me then and what continues to impact me even now, though to a lesser extent.

From the time I was introduced to the concept of sexuality until my wedding night when I first tried to have sex, my church culture taught me to fear sex, to guard myself against any sexual or sensuous advances, and to rebuff reflexively and deny instinctively any "impure acts." Sex was wrong, evil, and amoral. It was a gateway to many other sins.

Then, as soon as we said our vows and kissed our first married kiss, it was now suddenly perfectly acceptable for me to have all sorts of sexual experiences with my husband. I felt like I was expected to just open up, to overwrite all those years of negative sexual programming, and to replace them with a rich, healthy, mature, and fulfilling relationship with my sexuality and my husband's—all in the span of fewer than twelve hours. It sounds like a tall order, yet I had been led to believe it would happen of its own accord.

Some women make the leap or have the patience, persistence, and grace to build healthy physical relationships with their husbands over time.

Others like me find both our minds and our bodies recoil from our husbands' sexual advances exactly as they have been trained to do since we were teens. We have been saying "no" so long that we have forgotten or never even learned how to say "yes."

When we *do* try to have sex, our muscles involuntarily clench, trying physically to keep our husbands at a distance.

We experience pain and discomfort. For some women, sex is or becomes a complete physical impossibility.

The medical world has a name for this condition: vaginismus. Its vicious cycle of anticipating pain, experiencing pain, and trying to avoid pain (and therefore sex) continues until for many—myself and Rob included—it can come to define the sexual relationship.

• • •

As my marriage to Rob progressed, I often rebuffed his advances, and our sexual relationship was eventually whittled down to fewer than six interactions a year; it would happen then only when he would flat out say he needed sex. In those moments, I would agree out a sense of marital duty and obligation. My mental state during these experiences was deplorable. I would later share that the entire time, I would simply lay still and wait for it to be over, all the while feeling as though I were being raped.

It is critically important to pause here and point out that my now ex-husband is a good man who, like most husbands, simply craved a fulfilling sexual relationship with his wife. His expectations were reasonable, and his actions were not unloving. He simply did not know the extent of what I was going through because I had trained myself to conceal it so effectively in the name of being a "good wife."

The rigid mental framework of my upbringing led me to view sex as a duty I had committed to when I said, "I do." At this time, I truly did not believe I had the right to say no when it came down to it. I also did not know how to reframe and rehabilitate my perspective of sexuality so I would want to say yes.

• • •

More than a decade after our wedding night, Rob and I talked about our shared history, separated from the emotions by space and time. Rob chuckled wryly as he recalled the experience. "The struggle is real," he said, asking if I knew the scene from *Forgetting Sarah Marshall* where the newlywed husband forlornly shares how the sex is, "not fun and it causes anxiety." Oh, so true!

I asked Rob what it was like for him to go through those challenges and to be in that marriage to me for over five years.

"Being with that person, holding them, having that bond—it's another connection that is a very intimate side of things, and through the way you were raised, it wasn't treated that way. So much of that was ingrained in you," he observed.

Our conversation turned to the concept of "wifely duty," and on this point, Rob was very emphatic. "F- that! There is no wifely duty in my mind!"

All he ever wanted was to connect with me in that way, yet my baggage stood in the way of the connection because what he saw a means of intimate bonding, I viewed as a form of transactional rule-following that I was again perpetually failing to live up to.

I look back and wonder what we could have done differently. Would it have mattered if we had gotten more extensive premarital counseling that included a sexual preparation component? Should we have seen a couples' therapist right away instead of waiting until five years into our marriage? Should we have tried again with a different therapist, one who did not write me off as simply frigid when I told her I would be perfectly content and happy never to have sex again? Could my gynecologist have offered insight had I broached the topic and recognized what I was going through physically was not normal? Would it have changed anything if I had known what was happening with my body and mind and if I had understood why? Could we have somehow worked through those barriers?

We will never know, and as with any divorce, the sexual challenges were not the only failure point. We have both gone on to build rich lives separately, and when we reflect on that time, mercifully, we find we each have made peace with both our marriage and our eventual divorce.

Rob recently remarried to a woman he seems clearly meant to be with. I wish him and his new wife a beautiful, love-filled life together. He is a good man and deserves with her all the long-term marital happiness and fulfillment he and I were unable to find.

• • •

I only recently learned that I am far from alone in having had these sorts of negative sexual experiences. The authors of *The Great Sex Rescue*[7] explain some of the physical and mental sexual challenges that Christian women have faced.

When they surveyed 22,000 married Christian women, the authors found that in addition to higher rates of vaginismus, many of these women also said they struggled to engage mentally in the sexual experience.

During courtship, the women surveyed, like me, were focused on protecting their purity (read: virginity). They acted as a gatekeeper, constantly monitoring the escalating level of intimacy, ensuring they and their partners stopped before they went "too far."

After marriage, that now engrained, hypervigilant posture made relaxing into and enjoying physical intimacy with their husbands difficult. They were guarded, on alert, and ready to call "stop" rather than welcoming, enjoying, and fully participating in the sexual experience.

If you can relate to these and similar challenges with your sexuality, please know it's not just you. Those of us who have walked this path ourselves see you. We are here for you. We are ready to listen to your stories, to share our own, or to offer resources that have helped. You are not alone.

Ending a Marriage

In October of 2012, after eleven years together—five of them as husband and wife—I finally asked Rob for the separation that would ultimately culminate in our divorce a year later. Gracious man that he is, he agreed, even if it was not what he wanted.

Though our marriage had been struggling for years, I decided it was time to end it when I attended a multi-week work conference and developed a mutual attraction to one of my colleagues that I had difficulty walking away from.

I listened to Katy Perry's "Wide Awake" and Taylor Swift's "Red" on repeat as I processed the experience through journaling, including an entry from November 1, 2012, that reads in part:

> When I was eighteen, I agreed to something that I never should have. I was not ready to be a wife, to be anyone's wife, regardless of who they were.
>
> What I have recently come to realize is that I am still not ready to be a wife. Honestly, right now, I don't know if I will ever be at a point where I feel I can wholeheartedly promise someone that I will love and cherish only them for the rest of my life.

I was so afraid of judgment and recrimination from my parents that I could not make myself tell them of our separation. Separation often leads to divorce, and divorce is one of those major sins which reflect poorly not only on the child but also on the Christian parent who raised that child. Plus, in my small hometown, I knew everyone would be talking and judging. It was a mess, and I did not want to face it.

Ultimately, Rob jumped on that grenade and had the painful in-person conversation. Since it was close to the holidays, I stuck to making the announcement to our extended family and friends via our annual holiday news-letter sharing:

> *This isn't what we expected or hoped for from our love story, but not every love lasts forever. We both cherish the good times and memories we shared in the nearly eleven years we spent together. We do not know what the future holds and if this is truly the end of our shared story, but either way, we both wish the best for each other. Our time together has helped to define us each as individuals, and because of that, we will always, in some small way, be a part of each other's lives.*

Reflection Invite: Part 2

1. If I have questions, concerns, or a lack of understanding about certain teachings, beliefs, or practices of my faith community, these include:

    _____

    _____

    _____

    _____

    _____ .

2. When I had reservations or issues with my faith, I was taught to respond by _____

    _____

    _____

    _____

    _____ .

3. My religious community demonstrated love by _____

    _____

    _____

    _____ .

    This type of love felt _____

    _____

    _____

    _____ .

4. Have you ever felt unlovable and/or unworthy? If so, with whom did you feel that way and why?

_____

_____

_____

_____

_____

_____.

5. I felt abandoned, hurt, or let down by God when

_____

_____

_____

_____.

I responded by _____.

_____

_____

_____

_____.

6. The deepest spiritual or religious pain I have experienced was _____

_____

_____

_____

_____

_____.

7. When/if I shared this pain with someone within my family or religious community they responded/I imagine they would have responded by _____

_____

_____

_____

_____.

8. When/if I shared this pain with God, he responded/I imagine he would have responded by _____

_____

_____

_____

_____.

9. Within my faith community I was taught to view my body as _____

_____

and my sexuality as _____

_____

_____.

This affected me by _____

_____

_____

and if it continues to affect me today, it does so by

_____

_____

_____.

PART 3
LOOKING FOR TRUTH

*The truth is not for all men but only
for those who seek it.*

—Ayn Rand

CHAPTER 7
LAYING THE BEDROCK

In her best-selling book, *Eat, Pray, Love*, Elizabeth Gilbert asked us all—over a heaping plate of spaghetti—what our word was. If we were to choose a single word that defines us and introduces who we are, what would that word be?

I initially saw the film version of *Eat, Pray, Love* during my first marriage. It seemed a nice enough chick flick, but nothing more. It did not resonate with me.

Several years later, freshly separated from Rob, I rediscovered the movie. This time, I realized I was not alone. Liz understood what it was like to be the one who chose to end a marriage to a good and decent man whom you did not hate.

Liz also knew what it was like to be so defined by others that you had lost all touch with your personal identity. When she spoke of how she absorbed herself so completely into each new relationship, I realized I felt that way about my relationship with the church, my relationship with Rob, and even my relationship with the retail management job I had taken just out of college and was still grinding away at several years later.

In all those cases, I had come to be defined by my relationship with someone or to something else. I was a backslider, an apostate, a soon-to-be ex-wife, a dutiful employee, but none of that touched who I was for *me*. None of those labels defined the essence of what it meant to be Susan.

Who was I? What was my word?

I started asking the question then, but I would not connect the dots until years later.

My "word" is **Truth Seeker**. I am a truth seeker. I always have been.

When I was a toddler learning about the world, my list of "why" questions was miles long, and I took them all to my parents, demanding answers.

When I was five years old, and a friend said Santa Claus was not real, I asked the tough questions because I wanted to know the truth even if it hurt.

When the cacophony of doubts and unanswered questions about my childhood faith grew to an unacceptable roar, I sought the truth.

At my best, I have refused to hold back, to limit myself, to accept the status quo simply because it would be more convenient or more comfortable. In the end, a comfortable lie is a worse bed than a hard truth.

Seek to Understand

My band director, Mr. Boyd, was the first mentor I was blessed with in my life. More than just a music teacher, he also became a friend, a role model, and a stand-in parent I could relate to in junior high and high school when my own parents and I were quite distant.

Mr. B. engaged my questions. He encouraged my desire to seek the truth. He modeled for me, and for all of us who were in his band classes over the years, the importance of a ceaseless quest to learn, grow, and improve our understanding. Those who loved him say he "taught life through music," and that is the truth. Music may have been the medium, but for those who paid attention, he actually was a teacher in the messy, imprecise, challenging art of navigating life.

In his free time, Mr. B. was constantly reading. He consumed more books, newspapers, and digital content than anyone I have ever met. In a world where too many people are satisfied to let others tell them what to think, feel, and believe, Mr. B. never took the easy road. He did not shirk or hide from the big questions of life. There was no apathy in him, only a burning hunger for continuous learning—the ultimate modern renaissance man.

When Mr. B. returned from a trip to Cuba a few years ago, he summed up the experience in a letter saying, "Quite an amazing time this past week. I always enjoy having my mind stretched and ideas challenged."

I think very few people would say the same. Most of us would prefer to have our minds placated and existing ideas validated instead as that is far more comfortable and effortless.

Not that long ago, Mr. B. and I were sitting at his kitchen table, sipping chocolate martinis, and catching up on life. He shared with me a new after-school class he had recognized the need for and had received approval to teach. It was a logic class, nearly unheard of in today's high schools and becoming an endangered species even at the collegiate level.

In this class, Mr. B. asked his students to pick a controversial topic they felt passionately about—abortion, immigration, gun rights, religion, the death penalty, social reform—any of the big ones were fair game.

First, he told them to write a well-reasoned and supported essay advocating their position. He said the goal was to convince him they were right. The students easily wrote and turned in their essays. He accepted them then immediately handed out the next assignment.

"Now, write just as strong an essay arguing the exact opposite viewpoint. When you turn this one in, and I read both essays side by side, they should be equally strong. I shouldn't be able to tell what you personally believe."

Who does such a thing? Too often, we choose our side and then dig in our heels and refuse to budge on that belief. Very few of us do the research and gain the perspective necessary to convincingly argue an opposing viewpoint. Whether out of fear, arrogance, or disinterest, a part of us holds back from engaging the intellectual conversation.

"Seek first to understand, then to be understood," Stephen Covey reminds us. This, he says, is a habit of highly successful people. Covey's premise also echoes the Prayer of St. Francis which says, "Grant that I may not so much seek to be understood, as to understand."

Without seeking to understand others, we isolate ourselves within the preconceived walls of our own current awareness and perceptions. How can we ever grow or develop a mutually respectful dialogue with our fellow humans when we approach life this way?

Also, if we are too scared even to try to understand the basis for others' beliefs, how strong is our faith in our own position on any given topic? What foundation are our beliefs built on if we fear it can crumble so easily? My band director recognized all this.

While the rest of the world was busy loudly proclaiming their personal beliefs and seeking to cram them into our young minds, he stood alone and instead taught us not *what* to think but *how* to think. He knew we would make mistakes along the way, yet his vision for us was that we would grow into intellectually and emotionally intelligent adults. We would develop our own beliefs on a strong, supported foundation complemented with a willingness to understand and learn from others we met whether we agreed with them or not.

Mr. B. died too soon and too young. When he left us in 2019, I realized I did not even know where he stood on the important issues he had taught me to face. In all our conversations, he had never actually told me but had instead drawn me into a dialogue to help me explore my own perspectives and see where they needed development and further consideration. In the end, I believe he wanted it that way. He did not want his beliefs to sway those of his students who were still finding their way.

Guiding Principles

When I began my initial intentional spiritual truth-seeking mission, I made myself some promises that I recommend to others on the precipice of their own faith journey.

- **I will always seek the truth.**
- **When I find the truth, I will follow that truth wherever it leads, even if it is painful, inconvenient, or unpleasant.**
- **I will not deny the truth I have sought.**

I have since realized just how important it is to make these commitments, to establish these core tenants and guiding principles upfront, at the start of this journey before getting too invested in any one outcome. There is a reason the most respected clinical trials are conducted in a double-blind format, with neither the researchers nor patients knowing who is getting the medication and who is receiving a placebo. It is hard to negate our own bias. If we are predisposed to favor a certain outcome, we will naturally be more attuned to any indicators of that preferred outcome, and we may miss or discount signs pointing in an entirely different direction.

To offset the effects of our bias, it is key to commit to following the truth as we discover it. We make this promise to ourselves before we get started, and we come back to it throughout the journey. It is our anchor-point, our cornerstone, especially when we encounter truths that go against our existing bias. Without our promise, we risk only exploring truths which we already are inclined to believe while ignoring the rest.

CHAPTER 8
ASKING QUESTIONS

When I reached the tipping point for setting out on this journey of seeking truth, I was in college. The questions had been bubbling up inside for so long. Life as I had been living it with the beliefs I was carrying based on the convictions of my parents and the church no longer made sense.

It might have been scary to admit it, but I knew I could not keep living that way. It was time to act—to ask those big questions. It was time to grant myself permission to seek the truth actively.

I just can't do this anymore. I remember the painfully searing moment of clarity and realization. I was twenty years old, a sophomore in college, and up until that moment, an AWANA leader at the Baptist church near my university.

Prior to my freshman year, my dad had looked up what he considered to be a good fundamental Baptist church for me to attend while at college. As with the rest of my religious and spiritual life up until that point, it was not a choice for me. I felt no agency, no control, and no say over any of it. When he, my mom, and Karen helped me move into my dorm the weekend before classes started, we attended the new church where my dad made sure to introduce me to the pastor and other elders, plus get me signed up to be an AWANA leader.

Looking back, he wanted to ensure I was part of a safe, healthy spiritual community, which this church may very well have been. I was on religious autopilot by that point, however, and I truthfully cannot tell you whether this new church veered into fundamentalism and legalism or not.

All I knew following that first Sunday was that I was on the hook to attend both Wednesday nights and Sunday mornings—no option, and no getting out of it without some significant questions being asked.

On this particular Wednesday night, the group of kindergarteners I was a leader for were each coming to me one at a time to recite the verses they had memorized and to ask me for help learning the words to new ones. I would listen to them rattle off the verse, give them a hint or two if they were struggling, or send them back to practice more if they clearly did not know it yet. Once they succeeded in reciting the entire verse, or sometimes multiple verses depending on what page of their handbook they were on, I would sign them off and have them move on to the next section.

I was working with one of the little girls, teaching her how to pronounce a challenging word, when she asked me what the verse meant. I do not recall the verse in question, but the look in her trusting little eyes as she turned to me for knowledge is something I will never forget.

Our eyes met, and I began to explain the verse in words that made sense for her age while simultaneously realizing four particularly important truths:

1. The innocent little child in front of me would believe and internalize anything I told her at that moment. My answer was, in some small way, shaping her understanding of herself, her church, her spirituality, and God himself.

   She did not know what the words meant, and she was looking to me as her sole source of truth. The child had not yet learned that humans are flawed.

   She did not yet know that by asking only one person and unquestioningly believing what that one person said about anything in life, she could be allowing bad coding to be written into the internal operating system of her young, impressionable brain.

   The girl was sweet, innocent, and in a position to be taken advantage of by any authority figure with an agenda.

2. Fourteen years earlier, I had been that little girl.

3. Even as I was explaining the verse and giving all the "right" answers as they had been taught to me, I knew more than ever that I was not sure I believed those answers for myself.

4. I would no longer speak anything as being true if I were not personally reasonably certain it was so.

The next day I sent in my resignation as an AWANA leader, and I stopped attending worship services.

My dad called me the following Sunday afternoon as he usually did to ask how church was. I told him I had not gone. He did not seem to know what to say to that. He continued to call week after week, and I continued to tell him I had not attended church.

Finally, months later, the calls inquiring about my church attendance stopped.

Is Salvation Forever?

I started following my questions and seeking some answers in my freshman year before Rob and I were married. Four years later, in the fall of 2011, as our marriage was increasingly faltering and disintegrating, I renewed and intensified my search to understand whether I still subscribed to the beliefs of my childhood and my parents' faith. Terrifying though it was, I had serious doubts about how I had been raised, and at this point, everything was on the table. That included considering the potential that God himself was nothing more than a human construct.

It was horribly confusing and scary to be even asking these types of questions. I had been taught not to question, but I could not contain it any longer. It was as if I had been told to check my intellect at the church door and mindlessly believe it all made sense. I was to take it at face value believing it was good, right, and true, but I wasn't sure I could or should continue to do so.

In questioning, inevitably, my attention turned to the debate surrounding whether salvation can be lost. If I were even tentatively considering the possibility of walking away from my faith, I needed to know what that meant and the potential eternal repercussions if I were wrong.

On the one hand, I heard phrases like, "once saved, always saved," supported by John 10:28-29, which says once a believer is given eternal life, they cannot be plucked out of either the Father's or the Son's hands. That sounded like I could believe and then not believe, but once I checked the belief box at some point, I was covered forever.

On the other side, verses like John 15:6 seemed to say salvation could indeed be lost if you no longer believed. In this analogy, Jesus compared himself to a vine, believers to branches, and his father to the keeper who pruned the branches. He said if we no longer abided in him and were withered, we would be gathered to be cast into a fire and burned. That certainly sounded like losing salvation to me.

In our church, on the rare instance whenever someone did leave the faith, I overheard hushed conversations about how that person must not have been a "true Christian." It seemed that only the week before, they were a valued member of the congregation, a leader in the youth group, and someone who was assumed to be an "upstanding Christian," but public opinion shifted quickly. Suddenly their former belief was discounted and dismissed as never having been real. It apparently was not thought possible that an actual believer could move from true belief to equally genuine disbelief in God.

It all seemed like a bit of a cop-out to me since it conveniently bypassed the whole eternal salvation question. By deeming the parishioner as "not a true Christian," that meant they never had salvation in the first place, so they had nothing to lose. Case closed.

I do not remember hearing of anyone leaving the faith and still being considered saved, yet the concept of "once saved always saved" was still preached, perhaps to comfort those who worried about the potential of losing their own salvation. Years later, I dragged the phrase back out myself to comfort my mother and husband when they worried about my soul's eternal destination.

Trying on Ideas

For me, the first phase of the process was an information-gathering stage, during which I tried to remain as detached from the outcome as possible. The goal was for no investment, no emotional attachment—only simple information gathering.

Of course, I soon realized it was virtually impossible to be completely unbiased during the process, but the more we seek out multiple perspectives on the same topic, the more well-rounded our search will be, and the more we will offset our natural or learned biases. I was not there to commit to any single perspective just yet. Rather, I was browsing the clothing rack of spiritual beliefs and searching out pieces to investigate or "try on."

I found Belief Net® to be a useful starting point in comparing and understanding a bit more about the religions of the world, although in my case, the focus at that point in my journey was more on the question of the mere existence of the God of the Bible rather than the nuanced differences between various Christian groups.

The fact that it didn't occur to me to explore other viewpoints of Christianity is indicative of the legalistic church culture I grew up in. Our church's views of God, Jesus, and the Bible were the only correct ones, so in my mind, I knew all I needed to know about Christianity. I only asked whether God existed at all, because if he did, I already knew what was required of me.

Toward the end of my initial evaluation process, as I was getting a feel for what I believed, the Belief-O-Matic® quiz[8], while not perfect, helped me to narrow down a list of groups who potentially shared my emerging personal beliefs.

Throughout this process, I often referred to my initial list of the concerns and topics I wanted to explore, the points that had come up as I began questioning my faith. I wrote these concerns down, then searched for the best arguments, explanations, and supporting evidence for the various positions.

I also searched high-level phrases like, "best arguments for and against the existence of God." When I found a particularly strong justification for one position, I would then research the refuting stance so I could better understand the complexities, much in the same way as Mr. B would encourage his logic class students to do.

While other parts of the spiritual truth-seeking experience were more emotional, for me, this part of the journey was extremely analytical, as you will see in the next two sections.

• • •

I debated whether to share or leave out details on some of the arguments I personally considered during this time. In the end, I have included them as examples and insight into my process, though I ask that you please focus on your own questions and search rather than merely replicating or getting wrapped up in critiquing mine.

Arguments for the Existence of God

Among other things, I considered the cosmological first cause argument which assumes that every event must have a cause. The universe exists, and the universe cannot have been created from and by nothing. Therefore, either the universe must have always existed, or something outside the universe must have always existed. There must be an original first cause for the universe to come into existence if it has not always existed.

The second law of thermodynamics, or the law of entropy, states that a closed system like our universe has a finite amount of usable energy. Since this energy is continually decreasing, the universe cannot always have existed because that would require an infinite amount of energy.

Scientists have observed the universe is expanding. That means it used to be smaller and theoretically would have started out as a single point at the moment of the big bang. Recorded levels of cosmic background radiation also point to the big bang moment of the universe's coming into existence.

Since the available evidence seems to indicate the universe has not always existed, then based on the need for a first cause, something outside the universe must have always existed. The God of the Bible and the creation story of the Bible align with being this "something" that was the original first cause. From this perspective, the energy of the big bang would come from God's act of creation.

• • •

The origin of complex biological systems was another potential checkmark in the "God Exists" column of the mental spreadsheet. Scientific observations of the laws of the universe show they seem to exist in such a way that the constants of nature are precisely fine-tuned to support life on Earth.

The laws of physics and the probability of chance are stacked virtually insurmountably against the possibility of life existing on our planet spontaneously, yet here we are. This suggests intelligent design by a being existing beyond the limits of space and time as we know them. Could that being be God?

• • •

Finally, we have personally seen how complex functional systems like computer systems or robotic technology require external intelligence to create them—the greater the complexity of the system, the higher degree of intelligence necessary to create it. Since we humans are thus far unable to create sentient life due to its advanced level of complexity, our very inability points to the need for a higher level of intelligence than humankind for humans to have come into existence. The God of the Bible could fit those parameters.

Arguments Against the Existence of God

On the other hand, I also found convincing arguments to support the non-existence of God. The Argument from Locality[9] summed up my misgivings about religions having a strong regional component to them. It states that all religions, past and present, have a definitive and discernible origin in time and location.

That points to the likelihood that they are a product of their culture rather than a divine revelation that was only shared with a specific person, group, or nation. The way in which religions and their holy books tend to reflect the beliefs, values, and mores of the time they were written lends credence to the supposition of religions and their deities being human inventions.

• • •

Legendary stories like the Epic of Gilgamesh, which was recorded as far back as 3300 B.C.,[10] hold some interesting parallels to the story of Noah's flood, which according to biblical calculations, would have occurred around 2348

B.C.[11] In the Gilgamesh epic, the character Utnapishtim is commanded to build a ship that will keep him, his family, and animals safe during the Great Deluge that is about to cover the earth with water. Birds are released to help find dry land as the waters begin to abate, and the ship lands on a mountain after the flood.

The similarities to Noah's tale a thousand years later could support the position that Noah's story is simply a variation on the Gilgamesh epic.

• • •

Genetics were another sticking point for me. The topic of genetics has interested me since I learned the basics in high school, and the genetic problem of a single literal Adam and Eve from whom the whole planet was populated did not seem to check out from a known biological perspective.

Anyone who has bred animals knows incest leads to genetic problems like physical deformities or sterility, and the likelihood and severity of such problems increases as incestuous couplings continue through the lineage. How then could two people have been the source of all the DNA to populate the entire planet? What we know of genetics says that more variety would have been needed.

Also, would it even have been two unique sources of DNA? If Eve was indeed made from Adam's rib, her DNA would be identical to his, making the genetic problems even more insurmountable. This called into question the Bible's veracity for me since it seemed to claim Adam and Eve were the sole original couple from which all of humanity is descended.

CHAPTER 9
MAKING A DECISION

The burden of proof argument says the onus to prove a disputed point should be on the shoulders of the person making the claim. For example, if someone tells you a flying spaghetti monster is out roaming the cosmos and you need to worship it, it should be incumbent upon said person to prove such a creature exists rather than upon you to simply accept it and commence worship merely because you cannot disprove this pasta being's existence. (I did not make this being up, by the way. Just do an online search for the Church of the Flying Spaghetti Monster to learn more about the application of the burden of proof argument.)

According to this argument, if theism cannot satisfactorily meet the burden of proof requirement, then logic points toward atheism rather than theism though in actuality agnostic theists may still choose to believe in a deity while acknowledging the burden of proof not having been met.

People Will Talk

As I weighed the research and contemplated my decision, a Finnish phrase from my childhood came to mind: *ihmiset puhuvat.* Literally translated, it means "people will talk." In actual usage, it stands in for all sorts of worries like, "but what will the neighbors say?" or "what will the ladies at church think?"

Ihmiset puhuvat is the reason you take down your Christmas lights and yard décor promptly by the end of December rather than leaving them up until April. It drives you to park in the fitness center parking lot then walk across the street to the donut shop so no one who drives by and recognizes your car judges your proclivity for desserts over push-ups.

Ihmiset puhuvat. I was acutely aware of it and its implications as I realized if I kept pursuing the direction my questioning was taking me, it would lead to a place where there would be lots for those *ihmiset* of the church to *puhu* about.

To a certain extent, all children's actions tend to reflect on their parents, but in religious communities and especially in more conservative fundamentalist cultures, that reflection and its social weight are often magnified.

As I faced the potential prospect of truly separating myself from the beliefs of my parents, I recognized that whether I wished it to or not, the act may have implications not just for me but for them as well. Yes, people would talk, but ultimately, I felt I needed to follow my own convictions rather than pretend to uphold those of others. I only wished that my choices could have no bearing on others' perceptions of my parents.

Time to Choose

After years of questioning and months of intensive full-on searching, seeking, and considering, I felt it was time to decide. I wanted—I needed—to put this issue to bed and move on with my life.

The way I saw it at the time, if God existed, I had already committed to following him. I needed to suck it up and get back to white-knuckling my way through the grueling rule-following existence that was Christianity as I knew it.

If he did not, I needed to stop wasting time and restructure my life around the path that best aligned with my dreams and goals. Either way, I needed to stop standing at a crossroads making absolutely no progress in either direction.

I weighed the body of my experience and observations growing up in my church. I pondered the still unanswered questions I had about theism and considered the negative impact I saw religion having on the world. I noted the absence of feeling any personal connection to or interaction with a deity, as well as the scientific support for theism being a way to explain aspects of the world which we simply have not yet understood through science. I considered whether the burden of proof is on a theist to prove that something seemingly invisible and undetectable exists or on an atheist to prove it does not.

On a more personal level, I sat with the impact of what either decision would have on my life and my future. If God were real and I no longer believed, was the "once saved always saved" safety clause a "get out of jail free" card, or was I risking eternal damnation? If God were not real and I spent my entire life chasing him and trying to find him, what crushing regret would I later feel realizing my time had all been invested into a fruitless, impossible, and demoralizing pursuit?

It was hard, but in the end, I stepped forward into the life of an agnostic atheist and secular humanist.

Personal Belief Statement

In the winter of 2011, I crafted the following personal belief statement. It was important for me to write down where I stood at that moment in time, to preserve a snapshot of my current beliefs and reasonings.

I encourage you to do the same at pivotal moments in your own journey. Writing these things down helps clarify and document who you are today. It creates a tangible cognitive "snapshot" that you can reflect on later after you have continued to grow and learn.

My 2011 personal belief statement read in part:

I believe the purpose and goal of our lives should be to improve the collective value of humanity. We should each live our lives striving to create joy and beauty for ourselves and others. If we are wise, we will appreciate the beauty others have created, recognizing there are many different types of beauty and ways by which to create it.

If I had to quantify my beliefs for others, I would say I am an agnostic atheist and secular humanist. As such, I do not personally believe in the existence of a "God" being. However, this universe is a vast, unexplored place, so I must conclude that it is, as yet, impossible to know for certain such a being does not exist.

I do not believe in a literal heaven and hell. After our physical existence ends, I believe that since energy is neither

created nor destroyed, it may be possible for our conscious-
nesses to exist in another plane of reality that we as yet do
not understand.

As a humanist, I believe the "reason for the season" around
the Christian holiday of Christmas is to reach out to oth-
ers and provide warmth and light in their lives during
the darkest time of the year. Decorating our homes and
public places with lights and sparkling ornaments and
the giving of gifts serve to lift spirits and connect with
fellow human beings in a way many rarely do throughout
the rest of the year.

For me, Easter, rather than marking the crucifixion and
resurrection of Christ, is a time of celebration of spring and
the renewing of life in our hemisphere. It is a time when
we find joy in the return of the sun's warmth and in the
growth of pussy willows, daffodils, and crocuses.

Finally, I support the principles of humanism as put forth
by the Council for Secular Humanism.

Part of the reason for crystalizing our beliefs in this
written way is also as talking points for the inevitable conversations we will eventually have with family and friends.

For me, the journey of searching was a private one,
though once I had arrived at this place of new understanding, I shared my updated beliefs with Rob, Beth,
and eventually—several years later and in much more
brevity—my mother. My dad and I never really discussed
my beliefs, but I got the impression my mom had filled
him in, and he was showing me love by not forcing the
conversation.

Finding Closure

Also in the winter of 2011, inspired by the closure I had seen other former Christians gain through writing, I penned a sort of "coming out" letter which I shared years ago with Rob and Beth, though my family will read it here for the first time (with minor edits for clarity):

> *Even now, nearly six years after I stopped attending church regularly and four years since attending church at all, it is still a challenge to put into words my dissatisfaction with Christianity. Nevertheless, it is important to me at least to attempt to verbally quantify the reasons I have turned my back on it and explain the inner peace that doing so has brought me.*
>
> *One of the key problems I have is with the seeming paradox of a loving god and a vengeful god. It does not make sense to me that a being who teaches his followers to turn the other cheek and love their enemies as themselves would then turn around and kill thousands of innocent babies who had the misfortune of having been born to enemies of the Israelites or turn a woman into a pillar of salt simply for turning around to take one final look at the city she had called home as she fled for safety.*
>
> *Why would this being who supposedly loves all mankind (but still has his favorites, the Jews) tell a man to go to a king to ask for the release of his people who were enslaved and then "harden" that king's heart so he would not let the people go until the entire country had suffered through numerous plagues and the firstborn of every family had died? Did I mention that the enslaved happened to be the Jews, his chosen people?*

I do not see a reason to worship a being who would play with human beings and treat them as pawns in a game unless it is out of fear, and allegiance based on fear is not true allegiance.

Another key issue for me is that of guilt, blame, pride, and punishment. If something good happens in a Christian's life, the accepted response is to praise god and thank him for bringing the new job to you, saving your life after being cured of a terrible illness, money showing up just when you need it to pay the bills, etc.

God gets the credit—not you—for taking the time to earn a degree, research companies, network, write an outstanding cover letter and resumé, and show up well prepared for the interview. God, not the doctors and nurses and medical researchers who put in years and years of education, money, and time to discover a cure for your disease, gets the credit for your renewed lease on life. God, not the generous neighbor who slipped the money in your mailbox or the boss who knew your situation and gave you extra hours at work gets the credit.

When something bad happens in your life—your car breaks down, you lose your job, you are diagnosed with a serious illness—there are several prominent reactions among Christians.

First, your trial may be seen as a test of your faith—a way for god to help you grow closer to him through adversity. Hmm… in the book of Job, wasn't it the devil who god supposedly allowed to use Job as a guinea pig to test the strength of his faith because trials come from the devil, not the benevolent god?

So, either you're telling me the devil is causing heartache and god is sitting by, watching, and saying, "I guess this is a good opportunity to teach the little human a lesson," or you are telling me that god himself is making my life miserable so I will grow closer to him.

Neither makes sense to me. The former suggests that this supposedly all-powerful being has no problem with letting one of his "children" be harmed by the cosmic bully rather than stepping in, as a good parent would, to protect the child, and the latter sounds eerily like Stockholm Syndrome to me.

The second and personally most offensive conclusion reached by Christians regarding the reasons for hardships is that they are a form of punishment for some transgression. Who would want to worship a being who has no problem with striking you down with cancer if you break one of his "rules?" Perhaps those who fear that being's retribution. That was certainly a factor for me in choosing to leave religion.

Even now, I sometimes find myself struck by the lingering and irrational residual fear that turning my back on this deity means that some gruesome fate awaits me like those poor men who reached out to steady the Ark of the Covenant so it wouldn't fall and were instantly killed instead.

I finally decided, however, I cannot remain cowering in the corner of the cell, too afraid to walk through the open door because the jailer who may not even exist might catch me one day.

For me, there were two areas in which church teachings strongly impacted my life in a negative way. I am still trying to recover from both. First, the intense focus on repentance and feeling guilt for one's transgressions against an intolerant god found me locked in a nearly constant battle with crippling guilt and depression.

In the church, at least the segment of it that I grew up in, both of these were indicators that all was not well between you and god, so neither was something really discussed beyond telling the sufferer to examine her life and make amends with god.

The second area of ongoing struggle, frustration, anger, and indeed bitterness, for me, surrounds sexuality. When one is raised to believe the natural physical and emotional, romantic desires one feels for another human being are something to be avoided and guarded against until marriage, it sets the stage for a turbulent sexual future.

If you explore those desires, there is the immediate physical gratification linked to the resulting mental torment of guilt for having "sinned." Thus, sexuality on any level becomes something to say no to and reject.

How, then, are the bride and groom upon becoming husband and wife suddenly supposed to establish a mature, mutually gratifying physical relationship? Coming from this religious background, nothing in their past has prepared them for it, I would argue they are, in fact, more ill-prepared as a result of following the church's doctrine.

Premarital sex may lead to pregnancy if not prevented, STIs, emotional heartache if the relationship ends, and social stigma in conservative societies. However, taking the rigid position of abstinence at all costs risks causing young, quick marriages driven more by the need for physical gratification than readiness for marriage. It may also lead to a potential lifelong struggle with enjoying sex for those who adhere to the doctrine. That choice should be our own, not one dictated to us by a supposedly divine being who created humans with sexual cravings and then demands restraint from satisfying those same desires with which he endowed us.

Depression has long been part of my life, and Sunday afternoons growing up were always the worst for me. I would go over the fire and brimstone messages preached by the pastor in his big, booming voice and feel the intense guilt that I had been conditioned from infancy to feel over whatever minor "sins" I had recently committed. The guilt ate at me along with the depression until I was a 16-year-old high school sophomore threatening to commit suicide because I couldn't bear it anymore.

My dear friend, whose experience with the faith has been much more positive than mine, stepped in. as did the man who would later become my husband, and I was able to make it through. I would later learn that someone who has had one episode of depression is more likely to have another, and that has unfortunately been my reality; however, freed from religion, it has been easier to manage.

Another former Christian described Christianity in a way to which I can relate, likening it to an abusive relationship, and upon considering his reasoning, I agree. In this abusive relationship, the abuser (god) can do nothing wrong and is never to blame. Any trouble is brought upon the abused (us) by their own misdeeds. Conversely, if something positive happens, the abuser gets all the credit, not the abused. When the abused gets punished, she is told that it is for her own good to teach her to be a better person, more like the abuser.

I ask you honestly to consider if that relationship were described without naming the abuser, would you tell the abused to stay in the relationship, or would you be offering to help her run away from it? I know this—that is not the kind of relationship I want in my life.

The nearly twenty-one years I spent in the fundamental[ist] Baptist community hold some of my darkest, most painful memories, and for many years, I have harbored resentment toward my parents for being the instigators of that pain.

It is only recently, as I finally committed to clarifying my personal beliefs that I finally realized my parents had inadvertently introduced me to the answer all along—the vision of humanity and life purpose I can relate to and accept.

Gene Roddenberry's world of Star Trek, rooted in his secular humanistic world (or rather a universe) view showed me a place where morality can exist separately from spirituality, where purpose comes not from attempting to follow the teachings of a deity, but rather by attempting to live life in a way that allows one to add value, depth, and beauty to society and enjoy that which others have created.

I cannot change what my past has been, but what I can do now is find my way forward, taking comfort in the knowledge that I am not alone on this journey and there are others who have come out on the other side into the joy and peace of a world without a god.

To my parents, sister, and Christian friends: what you believe is for you to decide, and if your faith brings you comfort and fulfillment, then I am happy for you. I ask you to respect that this is not the path I was meant to walk.

If you are worried about my soul, don't be. If it makes you feel better, remember that according to your belief system, since I once professed genuine faith in your god, you will still see me in heaven one day.

Our country was founded on the basis of freedom from religious persecution—not "freedom" to choose between Catholicism and one of the Protestant sects, but true freedom not to be discriminated against no matter what one's religious beliefs may be. This freedom should extend to the right to choose to believe that no deity exists at all.

My hope is that one day, I, and others like me, will be able to come forward and say, without reservation, without risk of job or social discrimination, "I am an atheist. I do not believe in a deity. I believe our life right here, right now, is what matters and that we should do the most we can with it, so humanity is better, richer, and more vibrant for us having been a part of it. I believe our rewards lie not in some afterlife but in knowing as we end our life that we have made a difference in the lives of those around us and have impacted the fabric, the threads of their existence in a positive, beautiful way. That, more than anything else, is the greatest reward we can ask for—to have touched a life."

Reflection Invite: Part 3

1. If I have remained in my faith/religious community it is because _____

   _____

   _____

   _____

   _____

   _____

   _____.

2. If I left or considered leaving my religious community and/or my faith itself, it was because _____

   _____

   _____

   _____

   _____

   _____

   _____.

3. The questions I want answers to are _____

   _____

   _____

   _____

   _____

   _____.

4. I promise myself to _____

_____

_____

_____

_____

_____

_____ during my truth-seeking journey.

5. I will seek truth and understanding by _____

_____

_____

_____

_____

_____

_____.

6. When I find conflicting answers and strong points for both sides of an argument I feel _____

_____

_____

and respond by _____

_____

_____

_____.

7. If I believe God exists, it is because _____

_____

_____

_____

_____

_____

_____

_____.

8. If I don't believe God exists, it is because _____

_____

_____

_____

_____

_____

_____.

9. Record your personal belief statement. Share with a trusted friend, family member, or fellow truth seeker if you feel safe and comfortable doing so.

_____

_____

_____

_____

_____

_____

PART 4

LATCHING ONTO LOVE

Our better side wants to pursue truth wherever it leads; our darker side balks when the truth begins to lead us anywhere we do not want to go.

—Douglas Groothuis

CHAPTER 10
SEEK AND YE SHALL FIND

My path from gnostic theist to agnostic atheist was gradual. It was painful. It was filled with years of questions, doubt, and fears. Still, the process of testing the validity of my childhood faith was freeing in a way. The mere act of taking those beliefs down from their untouchable pedestal and allowing them to be critically considered rather than unquestioningly accepted signaled a new era of personal ownership and accountability.

If you are like me, what you also may be expecting is for the journey to be over once you have gone out and found the initial answers to your questions. The thing is that sometimes we come to the best conclusion we can, given the information, answers, understanding, and perspective we have at the time but that does not mean the book is closed. It does not mean the journey is over.

Our original process could have been tainted by our personal bias. We may have missed some important pieces of the puzzle. New, previously unconsidered information could be brought to our attention.

Like scientists who are constantly reviewing new data and seeking to recognize how it fits within or completely revolutionizes the framework of their existing understanding, we too must be willing to evaluate potential new truths we encounter. If we find we don't want to at least consider them, we should ask ourselves why.

In my case, the truth I am about to share was unexpected. I did not seek it out, but when it began revealing itself, I investigated the clues, asked the questions, and followed the answers. The process was at times exhausting and overwhelming. I thought I was done uprooting my understanding of the topic of spirituality. I thought I had done all the seeking, asked all the questions, arrived at the answers, yet new information kept presenting itself and demanding to be considered. This was the ultimate test of my dedication, of my commitment to seeking truth rather than blindly holding tightly to beliefs.

It feels only fair to warn you, as someone who has walked this path more than once, that there are times along the truth-seeking journey when you may come across a truth you do not particularly like. The "truth seeker" identity sounds glamorous, noble, and worthy, but when all your seeking runs you straight into a truth you were not expecting and do not personally like, you may want to give up and hide from it all. I know I did.

When new truths are triggering and touch those sensitive past-baggage filled areas of our psyches, that is where things get messy, and the allure of the whole endeavor wears off. Where we once were motivated, we must now continue based solely on our commitment and dedication to the truth.

Case Reopened

Two years after Rob and I separated, I had moved across the country for a dream job in San Francisco, and, though I didn't know it then, to meet my future husband.

We met at a social mixer—one that I almost backed out of attending because I was so nervous. I took the bus there, then hesitated outside. I paced the sidewalk across from the venue, talking on the phone to a college friend with whom I had been engaged in an ill-advised affair since splitting from Rob. I remember telling my friend maybe I would just skip the mixer and go to the mall, the farmer's market, or somewhere else less socially intimidating for an introvert. His reply seemed oddly out of place at the time yet felt important and weighty for an unknown reason. "Walk through that door, and you will never be alone again."

I hung up the phone and walked through the door. There, I met Mark. Six months later, on Christmas Eve, we said "I do." The night ceremony was private and intimate, just us, his best man, the photographer, and the officiant on a stretch of Hawaiian beach illuminated by tiki torches. My new husband was a Christian, but out of love and respect for my beliefs, he agreed to a secular wedding on the beach rather than a religious service in a church.

He did, however, gently and periodically encourage me to make my quest for spiritual truth an ongoing affair rather than considering the case closed as I did at the time. During several conversations, he mentioned numerous accounts of near-death experiences (NDEs) reported around the world. He highlighted multiple cases in which people had been clinically dead for a time before being resuscitated and during this interval, their consciousnesses had separated from their bodies.

Some of these people later recalled seeing details of what was happening in the area around their physical bodies while their cognitive awareness and sense of self seemed to hover above the room. Others met family members they had never heard of nor seen photos of prior to the NDE, yet their descriptions of these people matched the historical record. Some described meeting God or Jesus while a few spoke of visiting what they described as Hell.

Mark asked me why, given my commitment to investigating truth, I wouldn't at least review and genuinely consider how first-hand accounts like these factored into my existing spiritual worldview. I loved my husband dearly, and knew he had a strong record of having been proved right about many other beliefs and ideas he'd had. Plus, he had a point about my quick and reflexive dismissal being misaligned with my desire to understand. With all this in mind, I finally apprehensively agreed to at least review what others claimed to have experienced, though secretly I hoped I could find reason to dismiss the claims as irrelevant and move on.

When I researched first-hand accounts, I found that even author Ernest Hemingway had reported his own near-death experience when struck by a mortar during World War I. Hemingway later wrote to a friend, "I died then. I felt my soul or something come right out of my body, like you'd pull a silk handkerchief out of a pocket by one corner. It flew around and then came back and went in again and I wasn't dead anymore."[12]

After reading this and numerous other accounts, I reluctantly conceded that although the details of their experiences varied, the sheer volume of people from all religions and walks of life who had recounted some form of awareness and sense of "self" existing separately from their physical bodies was significant. Some of these stories could certainly have been fabricated or embellished, however it seemed unlikely they were all pure fairytales.

The circumstantial yet substantial body of near-death experience evidence re-raised the question of the existence of souls. Since the concept of souls is difficult to quantifiably prove or disprove through the scientific method, prior to this point I would have said I found it possible but not overly likely we had souls that would continue to exist after bodily death. However, the preponderance of evidence in NDE accounts suggested the need for a revision to that position.

Expanding the possibilities, I modified my belief to a tenuous supposition that we do indeed have souls, and these souls are capable of some form of electrical or energetic stand-alone existence following our physical death. Most people seemed to believe either humans have no souls or if we do, there must also be a deity who created those souls. But at the time, for no particular reason other than my personal non-belief in a higher power, I backed a third possibility—souls with no deity required.

I was earnestly and genuinely seeking the truth, but let's be honest: my search at this point was not without bias. I wasn't even considering the idea that the God of the Bible existed. In my mind, that ship had thankfully sailed. At this point in my journey, I would have much preferred the truth to align with New Age ideas that my soul was in fact that of an ancient starseed here on Earth to carry out an important mission to aid humanity or that "god" was found within each one of us and while on Earth our souls were merely on a journey to remember our own spark of inner divinity. Nearly anything would have seemed preferable to the narrative bound in the pages of the Bible.

Following the Clues

When we were growing up, one of the fun things my mom loved to do for us was to create treasure hunts for birthdays and other parties. She would come up with a series of clues, each handwritten clue leading us to the next, to the next, and the next, until we ultimately arrived at the final location where a pirate's treasure chest was waiting for us.

Soon after I had revised my position on souls to believe their existence was, in fact, more probable than I had previously thought, I began to consider other questions like *Who am I, and if I do have a soul, what is my soul's purpose here on this planet?*

As I was contemplating these questions a single unfamiliar word popped into my head. *Oolamee* – my first treasure hunt clue. I had never heard that word before, and online research yielded limited results, but the one result that matched the spelling as I had seen it in my mind was from the lyrics to the traditional Jewish Sabbath song "*D'ror Yikra*."

I contacted a representative for the band who had posted the lyrics online, and I learned the word *oolamee* was Hebrew. In the song it was used as part of the phrase, "D'rosh navi…v'oolamee," which roughly translates as "Seek or pursue after my people/nation/sanctuary."

Interesting. Why would a Hebrew word I had never heard or seen be what came to me in that moment of quiet contemplation? What did it mean for me, especially as it came nestled in the context of this song? I filed the word and its song away as a clue, feeling excited yet also a little uneasy about the whole situation's proximity to the being atheists sometimes refer to as "bible god."

Months later, Mark and I were spending the winter being snowbirds in our RV in the desert of Arizona rather than shivering through the season in a more frigid northern locale.

While there, we attended the gem and mineral shows where someone we met gave us my next clue: a small stick of light golden wood streaked with a caramel brown grain.

"It's called palo santo," he said, noting that when burned, the wood gave off a distinctive relaxing aroma.

Palo santo, I would learn, means "holy wood," and this unique species of tree is related to both frankincense and myrrh. The smell of the wood was wonderfully amazing and calming. Surely the name and its relationship to two of the gifts said to have been brought to baby Jesus by the wise men were a coincidence—at least I hoped so.

Unexpected Valentine

When I was growing up, Valentine's Day, like other holidays, was special. When this holiday fell on a school day, I remember opening my lunch box to find my mom had cut my PB&J sandwich into the shape of a heart. Nestled alongside it were a Hershey's kiss and a handmade Valentine card.

Many years, Karen and I would cover the kitchen table in a sea of white paper doilies, red construction paper, stickers, glitter, and glue, turning it into a sort of Cupid's workshop as we crafted Valentine's Day cards for our grandparents and friends.

Then, unexpectedly, many years later, I received my very own, personally delivered, handmade cosmic Valentine with a custom inscription from a source I had already concluded did not exist.

It was Valentine's Day 2019. Mark and I were enjoying another day of blissful solitude in the Sonoran Desert. For months, unbeknownst to me, my husband had been talking to God, praying to be an ambassador of sorts between God and me. Mark had asked for the opportunity and the right words to help convey a message of love.

On Valentine's Day, his request to be that "personal Jesus" I had asked for so many years before was granted. Remember my plea to be scooped up in this personal Jesus' arms, for him to draw me close, be with me, hold me, care for me, protect me, and love me with the most intensely beautiful, all-consuming love? It had been more than fifteen years since I prayed that prayer, but I was about to get an answer.

I was in the bathroom brushing my hair when Mark appeared in the doorway wearing an uncharacteristic look of indecision and apprehension. I thought I saw the hint of a tear in the corner of his eye. Confused, I asked him what was going on, and he said he had something to share with me, but it was religious in nature.

He said he did not know what to do because he had promised me not to bring up religion like this, and if he shared the words that were being impressed upon him, he would be breaking his promise to me. He did not want to do that and was practically biting his lip to keep the words from flowing out as he presented his dilemma to me. He waited, promising he would respect whatever I chose and would not press the issue.

At that moment, everything slowed, and the future seemed to be hinging on my response. I felt as I had several times before when faced with big life decisions the weight of which I sensed rippling through time and space. When given the choice to take a corporate job in Chicago rather than San Francisco, when I very nearly canceled on my first date with Mark, both times I had sensed that the easier choice, the more comfortable choice—the safer choice—was the choice I would come to regret. I was free to make it, yes, but it would be a choice whose effects and repercussions would linger long and bitter through my life.

Back in the bathroom, my hand frozen on my hairbrush, I felt the same weighty choice and again intuitively knew which answer to choose. I had made myself the promise to seek the truth. I chose truth long ago and ignoring or refusing even to listen to a new perspective because it might conflict with my established paradigm would be invalidating my very identity as a truth seeker. I had made a choice then, so I would not have to make it now at this moment when it would be too easy to choose incorrectly out of fear.

"Go ahead," I said. "It's okay. Go ahead. Tell me."

Hesitantly at first, gauging my response and commitment to hearing him out, he began to speak, and it was not long before I grabbed a pen and paper to record as much as I could.

The words he was led to share were deeply personal and private, though I will share pieces of them here:

- *You hate the truth, but the truth is truth. You may throw sticks; you may throw stones. Truth stands by itself. Truth needs no support.*
- *You have been granted a window of exploration to everything you believe in. You have been invited to explore the truth that is before you.*
- *Test everything so you may accept the truth. You were not allowed to test when you were a kid. You were told what to do. You didn't have an option. You are a tester. For you, because you need so much more validation, keep questioning until you feel free to investigate down to the core of the truth.*
- *There is going to be a lot of fire for you to walk on. A lot of dogma, a lot of stigmas, and preconceived notions.*

- *It is very important for you to feel you are not being driven, channeled, or boxed. You are being given, allowed to receive, all the information you need to make a sound decision.*
- *You have been hurt by the parentheses. You have been held by the parentheses. You have to tear down those parentheses—the block that is keeping you from reconnecting.*
- *Know that hate and ego were, have been, and are the parentheses that may and will try to keep you confined to your current reality. Question why you are thinking within those parentheses.*

It Is Time

Nine days later, on February 23rd, Mark and I spent the afternoon together sitting in our personal patch of desert listening to relaxing music and simply soaking up the tranquility of the day.

After a while, Mark decided to go inside and lie down. I was not ready to head back, though as he said we would have other days here. He hugged me and went inside, leaving me in solitude.

I stayed there alone for about forty-five minutes. Eating a protein bar, I watched as a hawk flew overhead. To the west, butterflies flitted in front of me in groups of two or three. A curving line of delicate spring grass drew my eyes to the base of the saguaro cactus before me. Time slowed as the sun prepared to set.

I was gathering up my blanket and portable speaker when I heard the door of the RV open. Turning to look over my left shoulder, I saw my husband walking down the stairs and coming toward me. His naked, darkly tanned torso reflected the warmth of the setting sun. The soft black sweats he was wearing were sultry and seductive to my eyes.

As soon as I turned to see him, I felt love. He was coming for me to hold me, care for me, and guide me back inside out of the deepening chill of the desert twilight. He jogged to my right then left, following the winding path between the bushes and through the washes. Back to the right and straight toward me now.

Even a hundred yards away, I sensed a change. In a moment, his energy, his purpose, his posture all shifted ever so slightly. It was nearly imperceptible, but one moment he walked alone, and the next, he did not. Another presence had joined him, and it was together that they traveled the rest of the distance to where I knelt.

I could feel the energetic signature of my husband's companion as they approached, and I knew it, recognized it, from our Valentine's Day meeting. My eyes traced their progress while some jittery butterflies took up residence inside me.

I knew who was crossing the sand to me, and I felt why he had come. I was nervous and in a floaty state of surreal disbelief that this was really happening. I watched them approach, seeing the movie unfold.

They paused, unspeaking, nearby, awaiting my permission. As it had been with the delivery of the Valentine's Day message, none of this would take place without my consent.

I drew a deep breath, embracing my identity as a truth seeker wherever that truth led. A wordless nod of my head and they closed the distance.

"It is time. I am here to bring you home to me."

The words were barely out of his mouth before inexplicable sobs racked my body. They came from a place deep within me, beyond the limits of my conscious awareness, and shot out unchecked and uncensored.

This time it was not praying a formulaic sinner's prayer. It was not raising a hand in a crowded sanctuary of bowed heads and covertly spying eyes. It was not walking down an aisle and going to a back room to fill out a decision card or talk to an elder. It was not crushing guilt nor was it obliterating hate; it was neither domination nor fear.

It was love—wild and raw and breathtakingly beautiful. It was kneeling in the desert before a gnarled saguaro cactus, the dry, hot wind caressing the loose tendrils of my hair, then being swept up in the strong, gentle, loving, infinite arms of my personal and literal Jesus as we shared an unspoken understanding and reunion.

It was being twirled around, feeling the sun and the wind on my physical skin while my closed eyes envisioned the swirling vastness of space, of nebulas and galaxies and the three of us spinning in an ageless, timeless spiral which I never wanted to end.

At that moment, I was inside love—nestled, cradled, and infused with a purity of love I had yearned for yet not believed possible since I was eight years old. It was a love beyond judgment, love beyond the conditions, and love beyond the caveats or possibilities of neglect.

"My sparkler. I can feel you. I can feel your sparkly soul," my personal Jesus breathed as our lips met in the intimate embrace of a kiss.

The moment reached completion all too soon. Slowly and reluctantly, we settled back down to Earth and to the realities of this planet, lingering in the dimming desert twilight for a few moments before gathering our things and picking our way back around the cacti and brush to return home.

CHAPTER 11
PROCESSING RELIGIOUS TRAUMA

If this were someone else's story—someone without decades of spiritual baggage—perhaps it would end here, nice and neat with all the loose ends tied up into a shimmering bow. There would be no confusion, no chaos, no angst, and no long path of acceptance to walk—just love, simply a pure, magnificent, sparkling, breathtaking love that wiped away everything else.

There would be excitement, awe, and joyful exuberance that wants to share this experience with the entire world. The story would end with an unmitigated celebration.

But this is *my* story, and this new chapter is tempered by all the others that came before it. It is *not* simple or neat. It is anything *but* easy.

Those of us who walk this path must work through our lives and our pasts—our relationship with the hurtful parentheses of our religious backgrounds—if we are to transcend them.

Where do I start? I wondered. *How do I even begin to process this experience?*

We drove to town and got ice cream. It was comforting—a familiar, soothing, everyday human moment in the wake of a surreal extraterrestrial encounter. As we relaxed into the creamy huckleberry flavor, we each, in our own way, contemplated what had just occurred and what it meant to us.

Part of me still wanted to run as far and as fast as I could away from all that had happened. I wanted to go back to the reality that had made sense before this event came along and shook up the snow globe of my life. Despite the intense beauty of pure, raw love and oneness that I had felt under the Sonoran sun, the equally intense ugliness of the deep, unrelenting hurt and pain of my spiritual upbringing was still just as real. How could I reconcile the two?

I wanted to dismiss it. I wanted it to go away. I wanted it to be a different truth, an easier truth. I wanted a more palatable truth that did not come cased in so much baggage. The truth I had found was not the one I had wanted, but I had asked for it, had I not?

And this is where the key to the whole journey, to the whole identity of being a truth seeker, comes in. Even as all these emotions and thoughts flooded over, around, and through me, there was really only one question I actually needed to answer. *Do I believe what I have experienced is truth?"*

Is it the truth? Because if it is, then the rest of it is all cleaning up afterward. If it is true, then I have already committed to following it, whether I like it at this moment or not. Theist, atheist, freethinker—none of that has ever defined me in the same way as "truth seeker," and it was that identity as a truth seeker I clung onto as I began processing this existence-altering new truth.

A Fighting Chance

As a high school graduation gift, my mother gave me a journal. It was the kind that had little quotes and song lyrics interspersed throughout the pages. The lyrics from Lee Ann Womack's hit song "I Hope You Dance" were printed inside the front cover. When I opened the first page, my breath caught as I saw the part my mother had underlined in pen:

"Promise me that you'll give faith a fighting chance."

I remember thinking, *she knows*. Despite my best attempts to continue going along with the expectations and portraying a good fundamentalist Christian teen who wholeheartedly believed the message, clearly, my acting skills were not as good as I had thought. My mother seemed to be aware of my doubts. Either that or she was simply afraid I would lose my faith at college as so many freshmen do.

We did not speak of it then. I thanked her for the journal and filed it away somewhere, never to be written in. It reminded me of the journal I had used from the time I was about ten years old until my freshman year of high school.

I can still see the blue and white rose pattern on the fabric cover accented with my artistic embellishments in metallic purple gel pen. Inside on the bottom of each page were Bible verses. Toward the middle of the journal, the verses are crossed out. By the end, they are missing entirely—torn out when I could no longer stand their words sharing the page with my innermost pain.

Now, many years later, as I sifted through the memories and baggage, those underlined song lyrics, and my mother's silent wish came back to me:

Promise me that you'll give faith a fighting chance.

Could I do that? Was I even capable of allowing that chance anymore? And should I?

What would it mean to give faith a fighting chance? I sat with those words and contemplated their meaning. Technically, to offer a fighting chance would not mean capitulation. It would not mean my former faith was being returned to that vaunted, untouchable pedestal of my youth. There would be no privileged position here, only the concept of faith in the ring sparring with bloody fists against the concept of—what exactly? Humanism? Some more nebulous view of a reality that simply exists without the need for a deity's feet to kiss and thank for it?

I wanted to deny this chance. Faith had years of chances. Fundamentalist Christian faith had the first eighteen years of my life, and its shadow hovered over me for the next fourteen. Surely that was enough, was it not? Enough pain? Enough torment? Enough wasted time, effort, and tears?

Except that something—someone—had reached out through my husband to talk to me. The words Mark had spoken that day did not come from him but were given to him from someone else. I could not, and—for the sake of keeping my promise to follow the truth—*would* not simply dismiss this encounter and pretend it never happened.

After following a trail of clues, after going through all the little checks and balances, all the improbable connections and circumstances I had experienced, I found myself faced with, at a minimum, the extreme likelihood that the God of the Bible did indeed exist, and he had decided to come personally re-introduce himself and tell me he loved me. On Valentine's Day.

The atheist in me thought, *well, there must be some other explanation. Your husband wants you to re-convert, and so he is just saying these things to get you to believe.*

The spiritual freethinker in me thought, *well, even if this is a non-corporeal or other-dimensional being speaking to you, perhaps it is simply using a name you are familiar with, and it isn't literally* that *God.*

The scared little girl who grew up within the rigid parentheses of the cold church of legalism began to cry. *I can't go back there! I barely made it out alive last time. Please, do not ask this of me. I cannot do it! I will not survive it!*

The woman who had already walked the exhausting, painfully searing coals of changing belief systems once sighed. *Not again.*

This journey of integrating new truth, of understanding how the fresh truth fits in with other truths or rewrites what we had thought were truths, can be hard and exhausting. At times it may feel anxiety-inducing, fear-triggering, and ego-challenging.

Depending on our circumstances, this part of the journey may call us to confront not only the role the church and other humans played in building up spiritual barriers, but also our own part in the process. It is not easy, and it is often not fun, yet it is ultimately freeing. It is worth it, so I decided to, as the military says, "Embrace the suck."

Was It Trauma?

If we had no baggage, no lingering barriers to confront, then the truth once accepted as such would simply be integrated, and the journey would continue. Instead, what we often discover is that the parentheses of our religious past hold our spiritual future hostage.

If the truth we find does not fit within the confines of our existing paradigm, yet we recognize it to be truth, we must confront the past that limits us. Only then can we move forward into the truth that liberates us.

As I began tentatively to revisit the pain of my upbringing and my own religious past, I faced the question, *was it trauma?* Looking back, it is easy to ask, *was what I went through actual trauma? Does it count, or am I just being over-dramatic as my parents used to tell me?* Many people who experience religious and emotional trauma endure physical and sexual abuse as well. That was not the case with me, so do I really have the grounds to classify it as such?

My husband is trained in cognitive behavioral therapy and other therapeutic modalities. When I am tempted to dismiss a childhood experience that clearly still has lasting negative impacts, he reminds me that what would not cause you trauma now as an adult may indeed have caused you trauma as a child.

Consider this example:

For most adults, if their beta fish dies, they simply flush it down the toilet and go to the pet store to buy a new one. Depending on the person, they may be sad, they may even bury the fish rather than flush it, but they most likely will not be traumatized.

When a three-year-old child's beta fish dies, it can be devastating. They had that fish their "entire life." They named it, they talked to it every night, and they fed and cared for it (hopefully). That fish was a key part of their world, and they feel its absence keenly.

The child may need to have a funeral for their fish. The parents might find themselves creating a headstone in the back yard, delivering a eulogy, and planting flowers near the gravesite. It may take a long time for the child to open up emotionally to another pet after having felt the bitterness of loss.

So, who is right? Is the death of a pet fish a trauma or not a trauma?

How often do we look back on our childhoods from the vantage point of an adult with decades of resources, experience, and coping skills, and then dismiss childhood pain as something that wasn't that bad? And maybe we are telling the truth in a way. Maybe it would not be "that bad" if we experienced the same event today. Maybe there would be no trauma. But that does not mean there was no trauma in the past.

Our personal thresholds for trauma fluctuate throughout our lives. If our experience at the time was traumatic, then we encoded the event as traumatic, and it continues to affect us in this way until we process and recode it.

We may also be tempted to downplay and dismiss our pain because "others have had it far worse." This may be true, but burying the trauma, invalidating the trauma, or denying the trauma does not make it and its effects go away.

That approach is like tying a dirty bandana around a festering leg wound, putting our biker shorts back on, and heading out to run a marathon. Just because the wound is hidden, just because we say it is fine or we pretend it does not exist, that does not mean our wound goes away. It slows us down, it keeps us from being our best, and it prevents us from running the race we are there to run.

Two children can go through the same event, yet one is traumatized, and the other is not. Why? Here is the thing when it comes to trauma: there is no universal criterion for what sort of event constitutes trauma because trauma is a deeply personal response. We each approach the world in a unique way, and that makes our experiences singular. Sometimes it is not just age that matters, but also those individual differences. What causes me trauma may not cause you trauma even if we go through the same experiences at roughly the same ages.

My sister Karen is younger than I am, so she was only four years old when we began attending the fundamentalist Baptist church. We stayed until she was twelve. She was exposed to the same messages as I was, and she was told the same things by the pastors, Sunday school teachers, and our parents. She was raised the same way as me, yet for her, this experience was not traumatic.

When we spoke about it more than fifteen years later, I wondered aloud how we could have so many shared experiences yet such different outcomes. Was it because, being four years younger, she was able to stay in children's church longer and accumulate less exposure to the hardcore fire and brimstone messages of the adult sermons? Perhaps, but what she said next surprised me.

"I knew it was wrong, so I just let it go."

She let it go. As a child, she somehow faced up to the constraints of fundamentalism, legalism, and pietism. She decided aspects of the model of belief she had been given were incorrect, and she would not internalize them.

"That's not what it's supposed to be like," she said of our experience of faith within the fundamentalist paradigm. "That's not God." In a way that I was not able, she isolated the manmade virus before it infected her.

Defining Religious Trauma

In her article, "Thou Shalt Not: Treating Religious Trauma and Spiritual Harm With Combined Therapy," Alyson M. Stone, Ph.D., CGP, defines religious trauma as "pervasive psychological damage resulting from religious messages, beliefs, and experiences."[13]

Pervasive psychological damage. I have struggled with perfectionism, a sense of self-worth that is dependent upon the approval of others, difficulty loving and trusting others, fear, anger, anxiety, depression, and exaggerated post-traumatic injury type of responses to a wide range of fundamental religious stimuli from certain cliché phrases to lyrics of traditional hymns. That sounds like pervasive psychological damage.

Resulting from religious messages, beliefs, and experiences. The religious message I received was that because we are all worthless, wretched sinners who are undeserving of love and connectedness, we must be working hard always to generate spiritual fruit and show outward signs that prove our salvation. I was made to believe that although salvation was by faith, good works as a Christian were integral to meet with the approval of both God and man. I experienced consistent long-term exposure to legalistic teachings that seemed targeted to break down my self-worth and fill me with insurmountable guilt, fear, and dread. Yes, it sounds like a large bulk of the pervasive psychological damage I accumulated was a result of religious messages, beliefs, and experiences.

Religious Trauma. Finally, there is a term that describes my experience, and perhaps yours as well.

Now, what do we do with it?

Assessing the Wounds of Fundamentalism

In *Dating Jesus*, Susan Campbell describes the lingering effects of her own fundamentalist childhood, saying, "The sword of fundamentalism broke off in us. We are Christ haunted."[14]

Before we can move on, we need to assess the wounds this sword inflicted so we are ready to begin the healing process.

Steve Smith of the *Liberty for Captives* blog echoes Campbell's imagery, writing about "trauma caused by the

Word of God used like the thrust of a spear, the constant threat of God's displeasure and eternal damnation, and the death of dreams and relationships." According to Smith, "This is real trauma—the trauma of the soul."[15]

Psychologist and former believer, Marlene Winell, has coined the term "Religious Trauma Syndrome," which she describes as "the condition experienced by people who are struggling with leaving an authoritarian, dogmatic religion and coping with the damage of indoctrination."[16]

Having been taught to see and understand the world through the fundamentalist lens from an early age, that perspective lingers with us and can subconsciously drive our thoughts and actions even when we no longer subscribe to a legalistic perspective. Like other traumas, each of our reactions to and long-term expressions of this trauma and indoctrination will be different.

For example, many of us were trained to seek external authority figure approval of our actions and choices. We were also driven toward the unreachable pinnacle of perfection.

At times I find I still feel apprehensive and uncertain of my worth if I am not receiving praise and affirmation in work, friendship, or relationship settings. A lack of positive and consistent feedback can spark the worry that I am not measuring up, which, if unchecked, spirals into a crippling certainty that I am a horrible wife, a miserable friend, a deplorable stepmother, and an utter failure in building and advancing my professional career.

As my husband unfortunately learned, disagreements could be especially challenging since fundamentalism taught me that everyone must agree on all points, or they could not be associated with. There was only one right way to think, believe, and act about anything—my way. The resultant entrenched mindset did not exactly lend itself to peaceful conflict resolution unless the other party was willing to continuously capitulate.

Abusive Relationship?

By now you may have noticed that many authors and bloggers who write about the traumas of legalistic fundamentalism have not only walked away from fundamentalism, but they also no longer believe in God. Some identify as atheists or humanists while others say they are exploring their spirituality. The God they knew proved absolutely impossible to believe in.

I get it.

During those first rough months following my desert encounter and subsequent intellectual re-examination of the case for Christianity, I felt as though I were being asked to get back into an abusive relationship. The God I had known from childhood was harsh—a megalomaniac, who as Gene Roddenberry put it, "created faulty human beings and then blamed them for his mistakes." The God I was raised with was limited to my internalized understanding of our pastors' depictions of him coupled with all the unattainable expectations of Christ-like perfection his church had pushed me to strive for and then chastised and shamed me for failing to achieve.

This was who I knew God to be, and this is who I thought I was being asked to re-commit myself to since I did not yet recognize how fundamentalism, legalism, and pietism had colored my understanding of him. I had reverted to believing the version of God I grew up with was a complete and accurate representation of the nature of the "one true God." If he existed, I automatically pre-supposed his character and posture toward me was exactly as my childhood church declared it to be.

At this point, the hope-filled questions that kept me going were these: "What if God is bigger than my existing understanding of the Bible? What if he cannot and should not be contained within the limited box of my preconceptions? What if there are more nuances and layers to the story than I currently realize?"

As I considered these questions, it seemed to me if the Bible was the inspired word of God and the love of God I had witnessed in the desert was also genuine, then perhaps it was my understanding and perception of the text that was skewed, incomplete, or flawed. Perhaps I needed to begin again, and this time truly seek first to understand as Mr. Boyd had taught me so many years earlier.

Cognitive Dissonance

Cognitive dissonance is one of my favorite psychological terms to talk about and one of my least favorite to experience, though I remind myself this period of discomfort often precedes profound personal growth.

The term "cognitive dissonance" describes the disconcerting state of psychological discomfort we feel when we simultaneously hold two or more sets of beliefs, thoughts, or actions that we perceive as contradictory. Dissonance is the sort of thing that churns around inside of you, demanding your attention, never satisfied, relentlessly badgering you until you address and resolve its source.

Other than unhealthy avoidance and compartmentalization of the conflicts, the only healthy way to resolve cognitive dissonance is to reassess and alter beliefs, thoughts, and actions as necessary so they all align.

Nearly a decade earlier, I had resolved my initial cognitive dissonance with legalistic fundamentalism by becoming an agnostic atheist. Now I was facing another round of spiritual cognitive dissonance.

There seemed to be so much incongruity between the patient, expansive, generous love I had personally felt that day in the desert and the harsh, micro-managing expectations of perfect rule following I had grown up with. I didn't know how to resolve the God I had met with the God I had been raised with.

In the interest of first seeking to understand the possibility of a more loving God, I made an active choice to hold the cognitive dissonance within me, unresolved for a time, though tempered by the assumption of positive intent based on the loving character and nature I had experienced.

It was a choice I willingly made to move forward, still without all the answers, yet not forgetting the questions, not burying or invalidating them. Instead, I continued to seek answers by approaching the questions from a place of love as I identified and processed the legalistic baggage that would keep me from doing so.

Fear Leads to Anger

When we were in middle school, Beth introduced me to *Star Wars*. Up until then, I had always been solely a *Star Trek* fan, but I found there were some interesting lessons to be learned from a galaxy far, far away as well.

Take, for instance, what Yoda says to Anakin in *Star Wars: The Phantom Menace*: "Fear is the path to the dark side. Fear leads to anger. Anger leads to hate. Hate leads to suffering. I sense much fear in you."[17] Yoda's words to Anakin may not have meant much to me at the time but considering them again now with the backdrop of my religious experiences, they take on a whole new tone.

The relationship with God that I learned from the pulpit of the fundamentalist church was fear-based. Accept God or else. Follow God or else. Do exactly what he says every day or else. Be an "on fire" and "fruit-producing" Christian or else. Follow all the rules of the Bible plus the added human rules we have set forth for you or else. There was plenty of fear to go around, and as Yoda predicted, that fear did indeed lead to anger.

I felt anger toward the church for instilling perpetual fear and trepidation in me. I felt anger toward my parents for forcing me to attend. Anger toward the pastor preaching those painful, cutting, self-worth damaging messages. Anger toward God for being such a micromanaging, manipulating, vengeful, helicopter parent of a deity who gave me life only so he could control it. Anger? Check.

Hate. This one I had to sit with and consider for a while because I was not sure it applied. One night while contemplating the question, I looked up the official definition of the word. Webster says hate is an "intense hostility and aversion usually deriving from fear, anger, or sense of injury."[18] Well, does that not sound familiar? Master Yoda and Mister Webster seem to be aligned on this one. Apparently, I absolutely had, over time, developed a sense of hate toward the church in general and the very idea of God himself. Hate? Check.

The end of all that, Yoda says, is suffering. To suffer is to be forced to endure pain or loss. I endured the pain of sitting through over a thousand fundamentalist sermons, many of them harshly legalistic, in the first eighteen years of my life. I missed the opportunity to develop my spirituality in a healthier setting free from the parentheses of legalism and fundamentalism. In internalizing a pietistic mindset, I lost the ability to trust, connect, and experience unconditional love.

Some of you reading this may have suffered far greater. Perhaps you lived through physical or sexual abuse. You may have been bound by more restrictive rules and regulations or sustained intense psychological damage at a formative age.

How do we heal from spiritual pain and trauma? When the roots run so deep, when the tree of legalistic fundamentalism has grown up, around, and through us, how do we extricate ourselves from its grasp without amputating pieces of our hearts and souls as well?

One therapeutic technique is to envision talking with your younger self or reading them a letter you have written about what that younger version of you is going through. We cannot change the past, but we can shift our ingrained perception and internalization of those events. We can process the experiences, accept what was, and find closure, meaning, and purpose we didn't see before.

I used to feel that to try to heal my younger self would be to invalidate her experiences, to silence her voice, to pretend it never happened, but as my insightful daughter asked, "Do you really want her to keep hurting?"

With this concept in mind, I mentally followed the root of my own suffering back, tracing it through the hate and the anger all the way back to its source: fear.

Fear is what has kept me from connecting. It has kept me from connecting with my creator, my husbands, my parents, and friends—fear of loss, pain, separation, rejection, vulnerability, and failure.

This fear was instilled in me; I was taught to fear. The seed of fear grew within me for decades, spreading its unhealthy and corrosive influence. But before the fear, there was pure understanding, connection, trust, and love.

I journeyed in my mind all the way back to when I first arrived on this planet. In that moment, I pictured Jesus catching and cradling me as I was born, filled with love and pride, whispering, *Welcome to the world, Little One. I can't wait to introduce you to it.* He held my tiny hand as I learned to walk and took those first steps across a sandy beach.

When I was two years old, I imagined him pulling me close and sharing that I was going to meet lots of people on this planet. Some would believe he was real and would follow him. Others would not.

Some of the ones who believed would say harmful, confusing things about him and how he wants me to view him. They would add their own rules and their own understanding to his words, but I would know better than to simply believe everything I heard. If ever I had questions or if something I was being told did not make sense, I could come ask him anything. I did not need to be afraid.

Write it Now

Initially, I resisted the idea of writing this book so soon, but the nudges to write it got stronger and stronger until one day, I found myself on an authors' webinar. I was on the call thinking perhaps I would get some ideas for another book I was co-writing when suddenly the presenter, Kary Oberbrunner, spoke directly to me.

In an instant, his words sliced through all the justifications, all the rationale for waiting until I had "more time" to process my experience and "more time" to gain perspective on it.

"The area of our deepest pain is often the area of our greatest impact," Kary shared.

Immediately my arms were covered in goosebumps, and the little nudge swelled into a clear and unmistakable message from an otherworldly source.

Do this now, God instructed.

But I don't want to, I silently replied.

Do this now, he urged.

I hesitated. *But I am afraid.*

He gently pressed. *Do this now.*

I begged. *But I am not ready.*

He patiently, yet firmly, insisted. *Susan. I need you to do this now.*

Physically trembling and sweating, my heart pounding, I finally agreed—verbally—my voice shaking as I said aloud, "Yes, yes. Okay, yes. I will do it. I promise. I will do it. I will write it now."

And so, the process began. I knew all I had to do was walk my way through the list of steps, and in the end, I would have written and published a book. I would be an author, something I had always dreamed of. The irony that I was getting what I wanted after all this time through having followed an apparently divine command was not lost on me.

Stages of Grief

Though, in theory, the book writing process was straightforward enough, the actual creation of the structure of the book was hard. I was discussing my frustrations with Mark one night when he inadvertently stepped on an emotional landmine, and the frustration and anger welled up in me.

"If God wants this book written differently, well, then he better come over here and write it himself! If he is going to co-author, then he had better show up and co-author!" I yelled.

My husband wisely took this as his cue to back out the door and leave me to my wrestling.

One night in the shower, after days of wrestling with the title for my book, I finally thought, *I'll know the title when I am given the title. Until then, I guess I do not need to know.* Immediately after relinquishing control and responsibility for it, the title appeared in my mind.

I started applying that same approach to writing the content of the book itself. *The words, lessons, and spiritual growth will come when I am meant to have them and not a day sooner,* I told myself. *If I have been guided to write this book now, well then, I choose to believe that if I keep doing "the next right thing," as Beth says, it will all work out as it should. If I just keep writing, keep learning, keep praying, keep processing the journey through the written word, then the timing and logistics will all work out as they should.*

Was writing this book itself some exercise, some practice in having faith and trust, in handing over control? You could say that.

Here is what I know. The process has been hard, and the non-linear path flanked with landmines. In most stories I hear about people finding God, their testimony ends with how great everything immediately became. We seem to gloss over or invalidate stories of those of us for whom the experience was different—more complex. Surely C.S. Lewis and I cannot be the only two who would initially call ourselves "the most reluctant convert[s]."

I talked with Beth often during the initial process of revisiting and dealing with the echoes of my religious past. She has continued to be there for me since our fathers set us up as friends in eighth grade. Even during her time as a Lutheran deaconess and mine as an agnostic atheist, she was always supportive, loving, and respectful of my intellectual and spiritual journey. She is now, as she has been since middle school, a safe place where I can simply be myself as I am at any given time without fear of rejection.

As I was talking with Beth about five months after the desert, I described how sometimes I had these really good days where I felt peace and love, where the words came freely and openly. Then I had the hard days, the days when I was filled with anger, resentment, hate, blame, and a level of ego that wanted nothing to do with any of this.

I didn't want to be wrong; I didn't want to be imperfect, flawed, and in need of anyone's rescuing. That was way too vulnerable a position to be in. It felt terrifyingly unsafe, and I recoiled from it.

Her response was something I was certainly not expecting. "That sounds a lot like grief."

Grief? Who receives a personalized message of love from their creator and has a response of grief?!

She was right, though, and I think Elizabeth Kübler-Ross and David Kessler would agree.[19] Denial, anger, bargaining, depression, and intermittent glimpses of acceptance—by this point, I had experienced nearly all of them:

- This can't be true. I already dismissed the possibility of the God of the Bible being real. **Denial.**
- I don't want to believe this, write this, or have anything to do with this. It's too hard and painful to deal with. I've already suffered enough! **Anger.**
- If I follow you, can I do so while holding onto some of my favorite current beliefs and without having to admit or own my past mistakes and imperfection? **Bargaining.**
- How can I possibly go back to being associated with the beliefs that have caused me and so many others so much harm? The God I learned of as a child is oppressive, and I cannot stand being trapped in that same religious box for the rest of my life. I can't live this way! **Depression.**
- ....**Acceptance.** I was nowhere near acceptance yet and couldn't even fully visualize what it would look like.

In the initial stages of this non-linear experience of grief, I seemed to spend much of my time with anger and denial while courting bargaining and doing my best to fend off depression. Acceptance lurked somewhere beyond the horizon, shrouded in shadows.

• • •

So, I was grieving, but what exactly was it I was grieving? What was it I had lost? Perhaps it was the ability to leave all of it neatly behind me—fundamentalism, legalism, pietism, the church, the Bible, the very idea of God himself.

I had put that issue to bed. I had stuffed it down and moved on, but now suddenly, the old wound was ripped wide open. I was faced with the painfully messy business of separating the proverbial baby from the bathwater, of sifting through all the convoluted trauma of my past, of facing myself and all my preconceptions, then somehow making sense of it all so I could move forward into my future.

Looking back now with three years of perspective, I realize that at this point in my journey, I expected acceptance to resemble capitulation. I equated acceptance with a return to my efforts to measure up to the standards my childhood church had set. I thought I needed to force myself back into the legalistic box with the self-flagellating pietistic mindset and acknowledge this box was what I deserved for being a horrible, worthless sinner.

The singular rightness of all the teachings of my church had been drilled into me so strongly from such an early age that I reverted to that mindset automatically without even realizing it until nearly three years later after it had almost crushed me a second time.

Take Me In

Writing a book this personal and raw has not come easily or comfortably. It was hard to read and revisit legalistic biblical commentaries and sermons, to articulate those old beliefs without the familiar feelings of shame, guilt, and anxiety washing over and trying to consume me with their ferocity.

Since the legalistic parameters of my childhood faith were so substantial, rigid, and pre-determined by others, investigating new perspectives and beliefs is also fraught with challenges that come from a difficulty with personal spiritual discernment. I never learned how to personally go through the process of biblical interpretation because someone else (the pastor or my parents) always told me exactly what to think and do. Some days I was tempted to simply give up and bury my head in the easy sands of legalism's cookie-cutter answers.

In the turbulent jumbled mess of other humans' interpretations and opinions spanning the entire belief spectrum, I felt as I did when Mark dressed me in a wetsuit and led me out toward the ocean towing a foam surfboard for the first time.

Walking to the water's edge, I felt confident within my own skin. The waves looked not so large, and I felt as though I could withstand the force they were about to throw at me. Once I was waist-deep, the peaks of the waves splashed stinging salt water into my eyes, and my board got pulled around by their power. I was in the messy, choppy surf zone.

My husband told me there was calm, peaceful, still water just beyond the surf zone. He reassured me that all I needed to do to get there was to duck beneath the waves and come out the other side rather than fighting to stay on top of the crests. "Duck dive," he said, explaining how ducks know that when a rough wave comes through, the safest place to ride it out is actually beneath it.

I never made it out past the surf zone to that still water where the real surfers perched calmly on their boards, soaking up the salty sunsets while waiting to paddle after and catch the perfect wave. My fear of the deep water, sharks, drowning, and the rough, wild, unforgiving nature of it all held me back. I was trapped in the punishing choppy place between the shore and the sea.

Some days it can feel the same with the process of confirming and integrating new truths. Life before those truths is the shore, the safe place of our former confident surety. Ahead is the calm, still water that awaits once the truths have been processed, but here in the surf zone of tearing down and integrating, it is wild and messy. It is exhausting and so easy to be thrown off course, to get beat down by the choppy waves of others' opinions, interpretations, and judgments.

The only way past that, the only way through the noise and chaos, is to duck beneath to the still, quiet place of direct personal prayerful connection that needs no external interpreter.

Throughout this faith journey I have craved that closeness, that intimacy, and I hear my longing given voice in the Kutless version of "Take Me In." I, too, entreat God, "Pass me by the crowds of people. Take me into the Holy of Holies."

This song becomes my prayer, my passport, my "duck dive" past the clamoring and contentious temple grounds, through the curtain, and into the Holiest of Holies where God patiently waits.

CHAPTER 12
A NEW PERSPECTIVE OF LOVE

One Sunday during the early part of this intense book writing journey, I was sitting at my computer listening to the Mormon Tabernacle Choir's rendition of "Homeward Bound." I had played this song repeatedly during the preceding few months, and on this particular day, the words drew tears.

As I sang along, my voice soared with the choir, and in desperation, I directed the chorus back through time to the church of my youth and to my parents as they were then. "Bind me not to the pasture, chain me not to the plow." Do not lock me up in this prison of legalistic parentheses and harsh, condemning pietism. Do not hold me here constrained and limited by the weight of all the graceless baggage you have piled on top of me.

I pled and called on Jesus. "Set me free to find my calling, and I'll return to you somehow." Rescue me, save me, free me from all the messy, ugly chaos and carnage of what others have said and done and convinced me to believe in your name.

Then come to me, court me, love me. Introduce yourself to me directly as you truly are. Let there be no intermediary, no filter, no human-imposed rules or regulations—only your heart and my heart, your soul and my soul reaching across the bounds of this physical dimension. Connecting directly, truly, intimately as you originally intended through your words where no one can taint or touch. Release me from the lingering guilt of my own failings and shortcomings. Let me soar free high above all that in the beautiful sparkling space of your forgiveness and grace.

Spiritual Kaleidoscope

When I was a child, we made homemade kaleidoscopes with paper towel tubes, cling wrap, rubber bands, and beads. It was great fun, but the kaleidoscope I remember most was the one that sat on my parents' friends' coffee table. I was fascinated by this elegant real kaleidoscope, and while the adults talked, I would spend what seemed like hours slowly spinning the dial, mesmerized by the way the colors and patterns coalesced and then just as quickly shifted again to form new miniature worlds of sparkling brilliantly colored glass.

The possibilities of combinations seemed endless. Just a minor shift, and the resulting image looked totally different, yet the elements it was made up of stayed the same. It was simply the perspective shift, the rearranging of the pieces and my eye's position to them, that allowed me to see the image in a new light.

What if our spiritual experience is like a kaleidoscope and our perspective is everything? Is it possible to view the same raw information—the same words, actions, and teachings of God from a fresh perspective and by so doing arrive at a new understanding?

In my case, given my overly legalistic past, I asked myself, *what would happen if I sought to understand God through love?*

Legalism tramples on the importance of internal, heart and soul driven love-based motivation for action. "If a man love me, he will keep my words," Jesus says in John 4:23. If you *love* me. The action of keeping Jesus' words comes from love, not the other way around. We cannot be legislated into love. The verse doesn't read, "If you keep my words, you will love me." Love comes first.

Love also begets love. Consider 1 John 4:19: "We love him, because he first loved us." Love, and subsequent following of God's will, are generated by the Holy Spirit working to rejuvenate the heart not by overbearing clergy enforcing a robotic congregational adherence to pietistic standards and telling us to love it. Should pastors mentor churchgoers on how God desires them to live? Certainly. Should fear and the ability or inability to follow the "rules" be what defines one's relationship to and status with God? Never.

A Table in the Wilderness

While working through my understanding of what non-legalistic Christianity looked like, I watched Rachel Held Evans give a presentation on the concept of biblical womanhood. She touched, as she often did, on how to her the Bible was not a blueprint or a set of clear checklist instructions. She said she viewed it as a "conversation starter, not a conversation ender."

Rachel embraced the uncertainty. She did not believe meeting God and accepting God necessarily meant that suddenly things were perfect, and we had all our questions answered. Rather, entering into a relationship with God was to Rachel the start of a lifelong journey of faith that should grow and develop over time.

In another one of her talks, Rachel spoke to her vision for what a church should be. She saw this church as a place where we would be safe to come as we are with all the flaws, the doubts, and the uncertainties. She encouraged us to bring our frustrations and our intellect. Rachel and her Evolving Faith co-founder Sarah Bessey invited us to a "table in the wilderness." There they created a messy, authentic spiritual meeting place.

Rachel and Sarah fall on the liberal side of the evangelical belief spectrum. Evolving Faith is a place of spiritual and social progressivism where many have found compassion and a spot to rest after being wounded by legalistic religion.

Critics note that while legalists have little to no grace to offer anyone, liberal communities hold an abundance of grace. They simply must be careful not to offer that grace at the expense of sharing the full message of gospel truth which includes the need for genuinely, personally trusting Jesus to redeem and rescue us, not merely acknowledging that he exists and he loves everyone.

Personally, I needed the perspectives of those like Sarah Bessey, Rachel Held Evans, and Nadia Bolz-Weber during this part of my journey. I was parched for a healing and sustaining love that was in no way dependent on my efforts to earn it, so I spent a solid two and a half years soaking up the words of those who wrote almost exclusively about the generous love of God. I needed to read the stories of others who were brave enough to admit their flaws, their doubts, their shortcomings even as they professed a faith in Jesus to redeem them.

As I first dipped my toes back into the scary, trigger-filled waters of Christianity, these women supplied a welcome respite, a nurturing spot to regroup and observe the genuine, honest, vulnerable journeys of others for whom faith had not been a simple certainty. Their introduction to the love that is meant to be found within the community of believers was invaluable. I am so grateful to those who helped me initially to envision what a faith-filled life could look like on the other side of all the hurdles I was still facing.

Listening to the conversations, experiences, and perspectives of those in the liberal evangelical community also allowed me to undergo a necessary personal version of "exposure therapy" to some of my own religious triggers. Before I could relearn how to hear traditional Christian phrases like "Brothers and Sisters in Christ" or respond to questions like, "Have you accepted Jesus Christ as your personal Lord and Savior?" without having a PTSD-like response, I had to begin with the baby steps of merely singing songs and reading books that spoke of God's goodness and faithfulness.

I listened to gentle sermons on God's love. I read books written by others who had lived and left fundamentalism. I wasn't ready to be thrown into the deep end of the theological pool or pushed off the spiritual diving board into the waters of joining a church just yet, but that didn't mean I lacked belief. Quite the contrary. It meant I was giving faith that fighting chance my mother had asked for so many years earlier.

Held and Pursued

Remember how growing up in the fundamentalist church, I heard about God holding us and how we could never be plucked out of God's hand? Back then I was not entirely sure how I felt about the idea of a massively powerful, cosmic deity scooping me up and plopping me in his palm, then peering down, presumably to inspect me for flaws.

Now as I view this image through the lens of love, I have come to wonder if perhaps when the big cosmic creator holds us in the palm of his hand, rather than scrutinizing and judging us, could it be that he simply wants to spend a love-filled moment admiring and marveling at his children?

Just maybe when he placed Adam and Eve in the garden, his wish for them, like a parent wanting to protect their newborn, was that his children would never have to grow up—that we could all be cared for, nurtured, and able to simply enjoy his creation without all the chaos and carnage, without danger and disease.

Could that be part of why God instructed Adam and Eve not to eat from the tree of the knowledge of good and evil? What if that direction was motivated not from a place of controlling domination as I used to think but from loving protection and wanting his children to remain safe even as he gave them the freedom to make their own choices?

I also used to hear talk of God "pursuing" us, and it had a negative and ugly connotation. In the sermons I heard, God was the angry parent chasing us through the intergalactic house so he could catch us, spank us, and force us to comply with his will. He was the warden out to collect the escaped prisoners. He was judge, jury, and bailiff hauling us in for sentencing.

When I put that baggage—those parentheses—aside for a moment and balance the perspective out by assuming a *caring* God is "pursuing," the context morphs. The kaleidoscope shifts and the image I see reflected back is one of multi-faceted love.

God pursues me as a gentle, loving parent who stays close to a child playing in a beautiful flower meadow near an unseen precipice. It is not a pursuit to control but to ensure the child stays safely off the jagged rocks below. He pursues me as a suitor, courting a relationship. He pursues me as a lover intent on sweeping up his mate and cradling her close for all eternity.

Communing with God

During those early post-desert days when Mark asked me if I had prayed to God lately, I often found I did not know how to answer that question. Initially, I would say I had "talked" to him. Then I tried saying we had "hung out," which sounded so cavalier and lacking in reverence. I still sometimes struggle to verbalize and to share such an intimate connection with others, even my husband, who is so close and precious to me.

The truth is all my simple words seem trite and inadequate for the rich depth and vibrancy of the experience when it is at its fullest. The word "commune" has been stolen and tainted in our society by associations with Warren Jeffs and others like him, but I believe it is time to reclaim that word.

To commune is to be in intimate communication with profound intensity and rapport,[20] and this is what I have experienced in those moments of solitude and connection. When I reach out and pray without ceasing, it is as though the Ark of the Covenant resides within me, and I pass through the curtains into the Holiest of Holies to a place where time disappears, and deep connection takes its place. I am within God and God is within me.

In that place, all else fades away. Hunger, thirst, discomfort, pain, the need for sleep—are all gone. All sublimated to the all-encompassing vibrancy of full immersion in the essence and presence of God. I can stay there for hours, sometimes all night, finally reluctantly slipping back to Earth as the first tendrils of the morning dawn illuminate the sky and my silkie rooster begins to crow.

As soon as my awareness fully returns to my body, the sensations are all there. I am suddenly and instantly ravenously hungry, seriously parched, wholly sleepy, and craving a date with my pillow. But mere seconds before, there was none of that. It was all suspended, and there was just God and me connecting and communing in love.

Reflection Invite: Part 4

1. Have you encountered unexpected or even unwanted truths during your search for answers? If so, what were they?

   _____

   _____

   _____

   _____

   _____.

2. When presented with new information or experiences that contradict my existing beliefs I typically feel and respond by _____

   _____

   _____

   _____

   _____.

3. If my current response to new information or experiences is not beneficial for my personal growth, I will shift my response by _____

   _____

   _____

   _____

   _____.

4. If my religious past negatively impacts my spiritual present and future, it does so by _____

_____

_____

_____

_____.

5. The religious memories, beliefs, teachings, and/or experiences from my past that are other than positive for my spiritual health include _____

_____

_____

_____

_____.

6. If I could, I would like to tell the person/people who caused me pain or trauma _____

_____

_____

_____

_____.

7. I wish _____ would apologize for the spiritual pain or trauma they caused me when

_____

_____

_____

_____.

8. Write out what you wish that apology would say:

   _____

   _____

   _____

   _____

   _____.

9. Have you experienced or are you experiencing some of the stages of grief? _____
   If so, which stages have you gone through and how would you describe your thoughts and feelings about each?

   _____

   _____.

   What are you grieving?

   _____

   _____.

10. If you believe God exists, do you feel loved by him?

   _____

   _____

   If so, how would you describe that love?

   _____

   If not, what do you feel instead?

   _____

   What could be blocking you from feeling loved by God?

   _____

   _____

PART 5
LAYING DOWN EGO

All changes, even the most longed for, have their melancholy. For what we leave behind us is a part of ourselves. We must die to one life before we can enter another.

—*Anatole France*

CHAPTER 13
THE MOST RELUCTANT CONVERT

Three years ago, when I first started writing this book, it was the last thing I wanted to do. As I reluctantly and begrudgingly sat down to write the first draft in the fall of 2019, I was, much as C.S. Lewis described himself to be, "The most reluctant convert." I had believed and accepted Jesus anew, yet my ego still wanted to grasp onto the straws of my own "rightness," of the correctness of at least some pieces of the custom blend of beliefs I had held to mere months before.

I began writing this book because I *had* to, not because I wanted to. Yet, for all my reluctance to do the writing, I *did* desire the spiritual growth. I wanted to continue following truth, I just didn't want to share that process with anyone. I wanted to grow in God quietly and unobtrusively. I wanted this part of the journey to be hidden away from public sight without anyone else getting to observe the process or have a say in it. It was too raw, too vulnerable, too unsafe and exposed to open up to bystanders. I was so embarrassed and deeply uncomfortable about having been wrong, imperfect, and flawed.

I hoped I could quietly finish and publish this book without much fanfare or publicity. Perhaps the book could be put out there into the world so I would have technically done my part and could move on, but that book launch could be as stealthy and silent as an unannounced Taylor Swift album release.

In retrospect, I realize my legalistic roots were on full display as I plotted to follow the letter of God's instruction to write the book while avoiding the heart of it which was to share my journey with others who had also been wounded by the church while inviting them to embark on healing, truth-seeking quests of their own.

Twelve Inches

In the fall of 2019, Mark asked our pastor friend to baptize him. Since he grew up Catholic, Mark had been baptized as a baby, but he wanted to be baptized again, this time of his own volition. The night before the big day, he asked if I would join him.

I had of course been baptized as an "adult" when I was ten or eleven years old, but that was during another spiritual lifetime. A repeat baptism made sense, but my first reaction was mentally and emotionally to recoil from such a public display of what felt like owning my "wrongness" in front of a gathering of our friends and neighbors.

As I went to bed that night, however, I felt a quiet, gentle yet persistent nudge and mental whisper that I should honor Mark's request.

I knew what Protestant baptism entailed. If I agreed go through with it, I would first need to talk with the pastor. Baptism isn't something you just show up for as an adult. Pastors want to have a conversation with you ahead of time to ensure they feel confident signing off on your spiritual readiness and the appropriateness of baptism at this point in your faith journey.

If the pastor in question had been someone we just met and had no history with, that would have been one thing. The thought of having that conversation with someone who had known me for nearly three years and who persistently had been praying and waiting for me to return to Christianity was another. My ego chafed at the whole idea.

Still, if I were going to be baptized with Mark, the conversation must be had, so I walked over to do it. Given my fundamental upbringing, I knew exactly what sort of questions to expect.

"Do you believe in God the Father, God the Son, and God the Holy Spirit?"

"Do you believe that Jesus is the Son of God and came to earth to die for our sins?

"Do you believe Jesus was raised from the dead and returned to Heaven following his crucifixion?"

Just listening to these questions brought up all sorts of deep religious baggage. I was not in a place to look the pastor in the eyes and respond, yet somehow, I managed verbally to reply "yes" to all these questions. It was almost like the Holy Spirit answered for me. I was filled with a sort of inner peace amidst the triggered turmoil.

The pastor agreed to baptize me, and I went home, relieved that part of the ordeal was over.

Later that day, I slid into a swimsuit and a flowy white coverup dress adding a cross necklace I had been gifted as a finishing touch. It was the first time I had worn any sort of Christian jewelry in a very long time. Before we walked over to the pool where friends and neighbors were waiting, I prayed to be able to focus just on God and not everyone in the room.

We arrived to see at most fifteen people, but it may as well have been a sold-out stadium. To Mark, the assembled crowd was a group of people who were there to offer "fellowship" and to cheer him on. For me, the experience was entirely different. I didn't feel supported by the onlookers. I felt judged.

My ego and church baggage came flooding in so strongly that they overshadowed everything. On that day, I thought everybody must be looking down at me, piously remarking on how wrong I'd been while patting themselves on the back for all the praying they'd done on behalf of my poor, lost, sinful soul.

I didn't want to be there. I remember thinking *this is the right thing to do right now, but I don't want to do it.* It wasn't that I didn't want to be baptized. I just wished it could be without the audience—only God and me.

Before we could go into the water and get it over with, the pastor wanted to say a few words to the assembled audience. First, he talked about Mark and his faith journey. Then it was my turn.

All eyes in the room landed on me. The pastor mentioned how I grew up in the church and so was familiar with many Bible stories and verses. He reiterated the questions he had asked me earlier along with my responses. I stared at the floor, self-consciously shifting from foot to foot, willing myself not to run.

The pastor concluded with a trite saying I had heard and despised in high school, though I never thought I would find it directed toward me. "The message finally traveled about twelve inches...from her head to her heart."

We entered the pool, and I was informed Mark would be baptized first since "the husband is the head of the household." Here was yet another sensitive topic from my past.

I have no memory of what was said in the moments before it was my turn. We have a video recording from that day, but I still cannot bring myself to watch it.

I do recall being so frozen in the strong, post-traumatic stress reaction to it all that I forgot to pinch my nose as I went under the water. I could barely keep from coughing when I came back up. I quickly fled to the side of pool and into the safety of Mark's arms for a long hug while trying to pretend that I was just fine.

"We prayed for you," one Bible study group member proudly and happily announced as we mingled around the pool following the baptism.

Her words made my skin crawl. Coming at the end of this difficult day, the seemingly innocuous phrase seemed to validate everything I had felt the entire afternoon. Even so, I recognized she probably meant well. I managed to nod, avoid eye contact, and quickly walk away. Still rude, I know, but it was the best I could manage.

I was relieved when the gathering dispersed, and we were free to go home. Although it was all just way too much, I said nothing at the time. I didn't fully understand it myself, and I certainly had no words to try to explain the complexities of my experiences to anyone else.

CHAPTER 14
FACING FAMILY

The first draft of my book was started in August 2019 and was sent to my beta reading team (thank you, Mark, Beth, and Karen) just over a year later in November 2020.

I made my updates and finally sent the file off to my editor in February 2021. It felt amazing to put the manuscript into her hands. I thought it would come back virtually ready to publish with just a quick final readthrough needed. The finish line seemed just over the next little hill.

As the initial writing process ended and my expected publication date rapidly approached, I faced the dreaded inevitability of discussing the whole thing with my parents.

My mom said that from her perspective, when I saw I couldn't be a perfect Christian, I simply gave up on Christianity.

It is true that within legalism, I couldn't understand how to be an imperfect Christian and still be a Christian. What sense did it make for God to expect perfection, send Jesus to die to cover our imperfection, but then still expect perfection from us afterward? In my mind, such a God must either not exist or if he did, he would be such a punishing, unrelenting, tyrant that I would want nothing to do with him.

Seeds Sown on Stony Soil

For those who haven't been there, it may be hard to understand how someone like me could go from a true believer as a child to an atheist as a young adult. I've asked that question myself the last few years, and I keep coming back to the parable of the sower, the seeds, and the soil in Matthew 13.

The second type of soil the seeds of spiritual truth can fall on is stony soil. Here the sown seed germinates quickly and sprouts up rapidly in the little bit of soil that is atop the stone beneath. Unfortunately, without proper water, fertilizer, and transplant into deeper, richer soil, the young seedling will inevitably wither up and die in the hot sun as its small roots cannot find life-giving water.

This, I believe, is roughly what I experienced. My childhood faith, while genuine, was not nurtured in an environment where I was surrounded by other Christians whose roots were planted in deep soil and who were helping me to cultivate that soil in myself.

I did not see the fruits of the spirit being produced in my childhood church. The church was much like the church of Ephesus in Revelation who had lost its first love. They were still trying to please God and to follow his laws, yet the loving heart of the Gospel was trampled by the legalistic application of the law to Christian life.

I did not feel encouraged to grow, so much as exhorted not to fail and if I did fail, to scrupulously hide all evidence of said failings. I knew all the answers but was unable to ask any of the questions. I was a believer but still living under the impossible mandates of the law, until eventually, inevitably, that law crushed me.

The purpose of the law as I now understand it, thanks largely to *Theocast*, is to clearly point out the already existing human inability to attain perfection. When the Pharisees thought they could meet the standard, Jesus leveled up the examples of what it meant to "keep the law" until it should have been abundantly clear that it is impossible to reach the level of perfection required. The obvious impossibility of legal perfection is supposed to drive people to the necessity of the gospel.

Instead, those of us who grew up in legalistic churches heard messages about how we needed to try even harder. Since Jesus said even our thoughts or the way we looked at someone could be sin, we must guard ourselves against all these obstacles. We were taught that as Christians, Jesus expected us to work hard to live up to his perfection and prove our status as his children. Obviously, we could never achieve the goal. It was an impossible task, and my tender seedling of faith bent under the weight until finally it broke, and I became an atheist.

The Way He Should Go

Throughout my childhood and teenage years, when my parents were attempting to mold me into the image they felt was right, everything in me reflexively pushed back. Though I internalized much of it, it was an intense, drawn-out battle of wills fought over more than a decade.

I felt my parents were trying to break me and force me to be something other than true to myself. They felt they were protecting me, steering me away from the spiritual cliff's edge, and guiding me to a safe and healthy path in life.

My mother and father's shared parenting goal as fundamental Christians was to follow the biblical mandate to "train up a child in the way he should go, and when he is old, he will not depart from it" (Proverbs 22:6).

I remember hearing sermons about Proverbs 22:6 and what I took from them was that this verse was a promise to parents saying if they crammed enough of God's word down their children's throats when they were young, those children would inevitably return to God and church when they were older—even if they ran screaming from it in between.

My independent ego drove me to hope whatever my parents believed was wrong. My parents were Christians, so all else being equal, my ego was predisposed to favor atheism. If my parents had been atheists, my ego would have been inclined toward theism of some variety.

My ego also hated the thought of my parents "winning," if I later came back to the church as Proverbs 22:6 seemed to indicate all church kids eventually would. I vowed never to return once I was eighteen and free to leave. I would be one of the few who somehow managed to escape, defying my parents' and the vindictive deity's control over my path in life.

For so long, I carried so much hate, resentment, and bitterness over my experience of those years. I have no biological children of my own, so I never thought I would have any personal experience in "training up" a child.

As a child myself, I remember wanting to have children someday. Then, without my realization, a shift occurred. By the time I was an adult, the thought of becoming a mother evoked in me an intense reaction of fear, claustrophobia, despair, and inevitable failure. My worst nightmares were those in which I was pregnant, and the moments of greatest relief came when I woke to find it was all a dream.

Through a beautiful and unexpected blessing, life brought me exactly what I needed to begin to work through this narrative, to better understand and empathize with my parents' struggles with the nuances and unknowns of parenting. I became a stepmother.

When Mark first told me he had a fifteen-year-old son, I was terrified. At fifteen, this boy would be old enough to judge me, to ridicule me, to hurt me in all the ways I feared. He would see my inadequacies and my glaringly abject failings as any sort of pseudo-parental figure.

Mercifully, the reality was far better than I feared, and he has had so much patience with me and my shortcomings.

We built memories together, from studying for our HAM amateur radio licenses to becoming EMTs. I will always cherish the conversations we had during his high school years. Still, for all my best efforts, for all my good intents, those beautiful memories are tempered by other memories of the times I projected my inadequacies and insecurities onto him.

We both remember the day I threw a dishtowel at him out of anger and frustration when he disagreed with a decision that I had made about how to pack up the kitchenware during one of our moves. He laughs now as he chides, "You threw something at my face." I smile with him, yet the memory twists sharply in my heart. It haunts me to know that in a split second, my internal frustrations, stress, and feelings of being disrespected bubbled over. It was that quick and easy for me to make a mistake and hurt him in a lasting way. I can only imagine how many similar moments people who have raised children from infancy accumulate.

During those first few years with my stepson, I often said how glad I was that my husband had a son, not a daughter because a teenage daughter was the absolute scariest prospect for me. I remembered so vividly the power struggles and competitive dynamics between myself and my own mother. I knew I had not yet healed from them, and I feared becoming a toxic mess of a parent who would leave her children with so much extra baggage to clean up.

Well, the joke was on me. I verbalized exactly what I was most ill-prepared for and terrified of, then a few years later, she appeared—an eighteen-year-old "daughter" who embodied all my deepest fears and insecurities.

Soon after we met, she "adopted" Mark as the lovingly protective mentor of a father she so deeply desired and needed. I had no idea how I would fit into her life, but eventually we worked through the challenges, and I became an adopted mother of sorts.

I agonized over how to show her love, how to guide constructively, how to protect her, and help her to grow. I failed and failed and failed again at being the "mother" I wanted to be, yet somehow her patience with my shortcomings was seemingly limitless.

• • •

As I prepared to tell my parents about my book, I thought back to those moments of personal parental failure with both my stepchildren and the grace with which they had each responded. On one hand, I wanted to show my own parents that same grace, yet all these years later, I still wrestled with the anger and resentfulness of not wanting to let them "win" by going back to the spiritual way they trained me up in.

The culture of the church they chose to attend had hurt me. It had damaged me and forced a need for the long and difficult journey of recognizing and working through spiritual barriers.

My anger flared as I questioned how my parents could have stayed in that church for so long, letting Karen and me grow up within the harmful world of legalism. How could they have exposed us repeatedly to those teachings and to spiritual leaders who modeled a debilitating pietistic mindset? Why didn't they protect us?

Even the act of publicly acknowledging the existence of God at this point in my journey still felt like capitulating to all the church of my childhood had stood for. Going back to God seemed inextricably linked to saying that my childhood church and my parents who raised me in it were 100% right. Returning and not departing from the way I had been trained up in felt like losing a decades long war.

I didn't know how to move past this barrier, and to be honest, my ego didn't want me to.

I lingered at this impasse for months until I was forced to confront it during an intense and difficult conversation with both my parents.

A Perfect Storm

The same morning that I sent the "final" book draft to my editor, I also emailed it to my mom. By this point I had awkwardly stumbled through telling her a little bit about the topic, plus she had read my original book proposal and outline, so she had an idea what to expect.

We both knew she was none too keen on my story being published, but since it was going to happen regardless, I thought it made sense to send her an advance copy. This way she could read it and start emotionally processing it before the book went to print.

I gave her a call to tell her the book was in her inbox, and I expected there to be only relatively minor changes based on the final edit. What she was reading would closely reflect the finished product. I could tell she was understandably apprehensive, but she thanked me for sending the document and we hung up.

About a month later, Mom had finished reading the manuscript and had some feedback for me. One of her most constructive critiques was that she felt the book painted all fundamental churches as fundamentalistic and legalistic.

Looking back, that's a fair point. The first two parts of the version of *Beyond the Parentheses* which she read were drafted while I was still very much in the anger phase of grief. There were definitely elements of pointed sarcasm and some blanket accusations which didn't need to be there.

I still stand behind my position that the church I was raised in *was* fundamentalistic and legalistic, but as I shared in the revised version of Chapter 1, it is important to highlight the distinction between fundamental and fundamentalist, so we recognize that some churches are simply fundamental.

• • •

Nearly four months after my mom read the first version of my book, Mark and I went to visit and spend some time with my parents. One night during our stay, my mom and I had an in-person conversation about the book and my childhood experiences in the church.

As we talked, my mom shared that she had not agreed with some of the teachings of the fundamentalist church. For example, she pointed out that Karen and I had attended movies and taken part in show choir and dance classes in high school. Such activities would have been off-limits according to some of the standards of our church at the time.

These were just a few more superficial examples of the disconnect my mom said she felt between what was being preached from the pulpit versus what she and Dad personally believed.

Mom's revelations were encouraging, but I still had follow-up questions: "Why would you stay in a church where authority figures were preaching all these things you didn't agree with? Karen and I were told to respect our elders and listen to the council of the leaders of the church, were we not? How were we supposed to know you didn't agree with the pastor on certain topics?"

Mom said she had wanted to leave years before we finally did, but Dad felt the need to stay. As if on cue, Dad walked in during the midst of this conversation, so I posed the same questions to him. Why had we stayed so long, and how was I supposed to know he and Mom weren't a unified front standing right alongside the messages of the pastor?

Responsibility, duty, and keeping promises are very integral to my dad's character, so his answer to my first question made a lot of sense. Shortly after we joined the new church, Dad became a deacon. When the pastor left four years later and the congregation was searching for a replacement, my dad was named as the head of the committee to lead that search.

The church didn't have much to offer to attract prospective pastoral candidates. Yes, there was a parsonage (a house owned by the church where the pastor and his family lived rent-free), but the job's pay was extremely low. Younger pastors with growing families simply could not afford to live on such a spartan salary. To make matters more challenging, the local community was small and rural with very few well-paying jobs with which the prospective pastor or his wife could hope to supplement their income.

After months of fill-in preachers and a revolving door of potential candidates, my dad and the committee finally found an applicant who on paper seemed like an ideal fit. He was medically retired from another career and would be joined by his wife as well as a daughter who was a couple of years older than me.

The candidate's wife was willing to take a part-time job at the nearby bakery shop to supplement the church's paycheck, and they said that would be enough for them to make the proposed salary work.

Given no other viable candidates, and the congregation's approval of the one in question, my dad and the committee moved forward with their choice.

I don't recall how the new pastor's campaign trail sermons compared to those once he was hired, but I suspect they were less heavily spiced with fundamentalism and pietistic wording than those he preached once he officially took the job.

With the new pastor in place, it became even more apparent that the church wasn't healthy, but Dad couldn't take his family and leave right away. He had been primarily responsible for the new hire and felt a duty to support him. Plus, Dad too thought Karen and I would both know where his and my mom's beliefs differed from the pastor's.

• • •

As my dad shared his backstory of the events, more than twenty years later, I could appreciate that he had been in a challenging position. He felt a duty to stay, and he genuinely believed this choice would be tolerable at least for his family as well. Still, I had to tell him, "I feel like you chose the church instead of your family. You knew it was an unhealthy church, and we still stayed."

Dad agreed it was unhealthy and said he could understand why I felt as I did. He pointed out that when they were making the decision, he and Mom had not had any idea how I was processing and internalizing the pastor's teachings because I didn't say anything. Of course, I hadn't said anything because I didn't think there was anything to say; I was supposed to follow the leadership of the pastor and my parents, who as far as I could tell agreed with him, but my parents didn't know that at the time.

As we talked, I learned both Mom and Dad had gone through their own spiritual coming of age struggles navigating a disconnect between their parents' religious beliefs and their own emerging perspectives as well. Dad had been raised a Catholic and Mom grew up Lutheran. Both came to believe differently in high school, and they verbally told their parents so.

Apparently, that was what my parents had expected to happen if Karen or I had problems with the church's teachings. Since they never heard that type of pushback, they assumed everything was fine. Instead, it was the setup for a perfect storm.

• • •

In emergency medicine we use the analogy of Swiss cheese to explain how if a series of circumstances and medical failures line up exactly right, the sum of the results can be much more catastrophic than any of the individual breakdowns on their own. When multiple failures stack on top of each other, the patient "falls through the holes" of the system, often with a fatal or near-fatal outcome.

In my world, the holes of desire for parental approval, learned and innate perfectionism, egoism, legalism, fundamentalism, and pietism had all aligned to create and foster an environment where it felt unsafe to be vulnerable, to ask questions, or to voice pain. Despite all I had been going through, my parents genuinely had no idea because I didn't feel safe to have that type of conversation with them.

Having a version of that conversation twenty years later was still emotionally draining and intimidating. It still didn't feel safe, but this time I was giving my younger self back her voice. I was advocating for her as she had been unable to advocate for herself. It didn't suddenly make everything better, but it was a healthy start.

My experience with my own "parental" missteps and imperfections has also softened the expectations I have for my parents. Like most who find themselves in that role, they did the best they could with what they had and what they knew. They weren't perfect, but the truth is, none of us are. Sometimes all we can hope for is to do the best we can, leading from a place of love and for our children to extend us grace when we too inevitably fall short of parental perfection.

CHAPTER 15
ADMITTING HUMANITY

Most of us see or at least want to see ourselves as the hero in our own story and I certainly felt that way about my spiritual journey. I wanted to be able to trust my instincts and intuition. Being wrong scared me. If I could be wrong about something as significant as the existence and nature of the creator of the universe, how many hundreds of other less critical things am I wrong about every single day of my life?

Once I realized I would have to admit being wrong about God, in classic victim mentality, I at the very least wanted to be able to blame the origin of all that wrongness on others rather than shouldering any of the responsibility for myself. My therapist friend, Shannon, explains, "The ego can't handle being wrong and it will do whatever or ignore whatever it takes in order not to experience that wrongness."

I believe Eckhart Tolle was correct when he cautioned against falling into the ego trap of continuing to live within and be defined by negative aspects of our past. Tolle shared, "If no one will listen to my sad story, I can tell it to myself in my head, over and over, and feel sorry for myself, and so have an identity as someone who is being treated unfairly by life or other people, fate or God. It gives definition to my self-image, makes me into someone, and that is all that matters to the ego."

Mark called me on it. I *did*, as he pointed out, want to write this book as though my "shi*" didn't stink. In the hero's journey arc, my ego called for me to come out the victor, the one who faced the trials and temptations but didn't succumb to them. I wanted to be the one who rose victorious from the battle, the one who never failed. Yet Mark kept asking me, "When are you going to forgive yourself for being human like the rest of us?"

Spiritual Hypochondria

I didn't realize it at the time, but the strong negative response I had the day of my second baptism would come back to affect me again in an even bigger way more than a year and a half later.

It all came to a head the night before my thirty-fifth birthday as I was pushing hard on what I thought were the final book edits needed to complete the already overdue finished work.

The more I re-read the manuscript however, the rougher it felt and the less confident I was about the whole project. The book just wasn't coming together as it should. More and more pieces stood out as needing to be fixed or even eliminated altogether.

The parts I had written smacked uncomfortably of ego. They were worded as though I again had all the answers, but I was starting to realize I still had plenty of questions.

Although I was praying for God's help and guidance in the process, I felt spiritually abandoned and attacked. The whole project seemed insurmountable.

I tried to explain it to Mark, but I couldn't fully understand it myself. I had no words to articulate what I was going through, and I felt like a crazy spiritual hypochondriac consumed by fear, anxiety, guilt, and depression. I was questioning and worrying about everything, yet it was all so nebulous I couldn't seem to grasp it and pinpoint the root of the problem.

It wasn't until more than six months later that I finally got enough perspective to have a better idea of what had been happening during this challenging and terrifying time.

Let's go back to the day of the baptism. As I now understand it, my response was triggered both by religious baggage and my ego feeling threatened by publicly having to admit being wrong about God. But I didn't realize this at the time. Instead, my pietistic mindset triggered concern that such a response must mean I either didn't really believe or didn't truly love God.

Legalism simply reinforced the pietistic fearful misgivings by agreeing and pointing out that my inability to write the book I had been called to write was indicative of a lack of bearing spiritual fruit, thus I may not be saved. Then religious fear and spiritual hypochondria took over to shove me down a rabbit hole of questioning what unforgivable sin I must have committed to land me in a position from which I could not be rescued.

My anxious brain chimed in "helpfully" to suggest perhaps I was somehow possessed by demons but didn't realize it and *that* was what was causing all my problems. Such a response sounds extreme, I know, but anxiety is happy to drag up all sorts of terrifying possibilities to ensnare and consume our minds. It's a dark, lonely, terrifying place to be, and unless a person has been there or has experience helping others walk that road, it is nearly impossible to understand.

The only way out of this dark place was by clinging to the promise of God's forgiveness, justification, and redemption of those who diligently seek him. The love of God was a life preserver keeping me afloat in a sea of doubt and fear. "Return unto me, and I will return unto you," he said to his people in Malachi 3:7 after they had already knowingly worshipped and offered sacrifices to false gods. "And ye shall seek me, and find me, when ye shall search for me with all your heart," he promised the Israelites in Jeremiah 29:13.

If after all the horrible things his people had done, God was not only willing but eager to call them back home to him, would his heart toward me really be so different? Would he not rescue and redeem me too from all evil if I trusted him to do so?

Searching for Answers

I did more online research during this time, some of which only served to fuel my anxiety, but other portions of which were immensely helpful. I discovered *Theocast* and the pastors there gave me the vocabulary and perspective to begin understanding what was going on in my brain.

The pitfalls and challenges I was experiencing were normal for someone who had lived the experiences and developed the mindset I had. I was not alone in this journey from legalistic, pietistic fundamentalism into a more healthy, genuine personal relationship with God. Others had also survived walking this path, some of them even stopping at atheism in between as I did.

Though I read others' perspectives both in books and online, I did not reach out in person since I often feel as though I should be able to do everything on my own with no support from others.

To ask for help or to admit an inability to accomplish something on my own feels weak. In my mind, I'm supposed to be able to follow all the rules, excel at all the challenges, and accomplish all the amazing things with no backup, training, or mentorship from anyone. Why? Because anything less would be to admit my humanity.

Asking for Help

Eventually, after several weeks of private, intense internal turmoil, I opened up to Mark about what I was going through. He encouraged me to reach out to Karen and Beth asking for prayer for the rewriting process.

I emailed and texted them. It was easier than calling, though as I wrote the initial emails, I still cringed with discomfort. I realized I never before had asked someone to pray for me. In my mind, prayer requests were for weak Christians who couldn't handle life on their own or who needed reinforcement because they weren't sure God was hearing their prayers. But here I was—asking for prayer.

At this same time, in the weeks following my birthday, I started daily Bible studies through a Bible app. Mark and I also began reading the Bible together each night. Until then, my past baggage had made Bible study of any kind difficult. I would read the words but automatically apply legalistic interpretations and understandings of them or be reminded of times when those types of interpretations had been forced on me. Plus, my ego bristled at any verses relating to surrender, submission, obedience, and similar concepts.

On the sixty-ninth day, after nine straight weeks of prayer, reading, and studying, on the morning the new outline and focus of the book came together, the fitting verse of the day in my Bible app was Matthew 7:7 "Ask, and it shall be given you; seek, and ye shall find; knock, and it shall be opened unto you:"

Authentic Apology to Self

I was mere weeks away from the already extended publication deadline for my book and was now facing an extensive re-write. I knew I wouldn't make it, and the weight of yet another failure pressed down on me.

By this point I had recognized the excessive ego-driven victim mentality that the last draft of my book was steeped in, but no matter how much I tried, I could not seem to find the way to move past it. I was stuck, both with the book and with the next stage of healing and spiritual growth, so I did as Mark suggested and reached out to Shannon.

I told her how, as I was re-reading my book after having been in the process of writing it for over two years, I was noticing themes of ego and of not wanting to admit having been wrong.

"You grow, you learn, you change, and you see things perhaps a little differently than you did when you first started writing something," I explained. "That's definitely a big piece of why these edits are taking so long and why I've been struggling with this so much—the ego and not wanting to own what parts I was culpable for. There is the instinct to put everything on someone else. I'm not saying that parts of it don't belong with someone else but being able to own the parts that I screwed up is a struggle."

Shannon replied, "Living in that truth and stepping into that truth is a process as well that involves addressing our ego, owning that we were wrong about something, and forgiving ourselves for that wrongness so we can be free of the guilt and shame of failure."

She continued, "There needs to be a lot of work around forgiveness and acceptance. What does it really mean to be sorry? The ego somehow equates apologizing to negating its existence, but one of the most powerful tools in humanity is a sincere and authentic apology. That's what someone must do when cognitive dissonance has kept them from truth and authenticity for so long. They need to be able to explore an authentic apology to self and then likely to others that they put walls up with or blocked and that sort of thing."

Shannon was right of course, and I recognized it immediately, but the question was, could I do it? I had admitted to God that I was wrong and had asked him to forgive me, but could I extend myself the same forgiveness? What would that "authentic apology to self" look like?

Reflection Invite: Part 5

1. Are you able to acknowledge and own the times when you have been wrong or have made a spiritual mistake?

   _____

   _____

2. Looking back, a spiritual mistake that lingers with me was when I _____

   _____

   _____.

3. I feel _____ about this mistake because

   _____

   _____

   _____.

4. If I could do it over again, I would _____

   _____

   _____

   _____.

5. Are you able to forgive yourself for being wrong or making those mistakes?

   _____

   _____

6. If you can forgive yourself, write out or record your apology to self.

_____

_____

_____

_____

_____

_____

_____

_____

_____

_____

_____

7. If you are unable to forgive, what is holding you back from making an authentic apology to self?

_____

_____

_____

_____

8. What steps can you see yourself taking to work past this block?

_____

_____

_____

_____

PART 6

LETTING GO OF PERFECTIONISM

"At its root, perfectionism isn't really about a deep love of being meticulous. It's about fear. Fear of making a mistake. Fear of disappointing others. Fear of failure. Fear of success."

—Michael Law

CHAPTER 16
HIDING FROM IMPERFECTION

After the conversation with Shannon, I still thought the journey was nearly over. All I needed to do was to read back through my manuscript, acknowledge and weed out those elements of ego, and the book would be done. I could forgive myself and move on.

I forgot that when our egos assert themselves, it is in an effort to protect us from a perceived threat. When ego recognizes a danger to our sense of self, it lashes out and puts up barriers. By consciously choosing to dismantle the protective barrier of the ego and admit my "wrongness," I unknowingly exposed the set of parentheses that was hiding beneath: perfectionism.

Before I could really lay down my ego and forgive myself, as Shannon had said, I needed to feel safe to be wrong in the first place. We won't be free to let go of perfectionism until we feel safe to make a mistake, safe to fail, safe to apologize. We need to know we are safe both to *be* imperfect and to acknowledge that imperfection.

It took a lot to convince me I was not and never would be perfect on my own. The Israelites wandered in the desert forty years. I wandered in the wilderness for a little over seven, and in that time, I racked up plenty of proof of my own imperfection.

Two years after the desert, I had worked through so much of the old religious baggage, yet I still did not feel safe to be imperfect. Originally, my ego had been "protecting" me from the perceived consequences of imperfection. As I began the work to acknowledge my "wrongness" and forgive myself for it, however, I could no longer hide. My now naked and exposed inability to be perfect began fueling all sorts of emotions as evidenced by my updated description of the depression stage of grief:

> *"I have made so many ugly mistakes. I have failed repeatedly at achieving sinless perfection. I'm consumed with guilt, anxiety, and fear."*

Striving Veneer of Perfection

In my mind, the very worst thing someone can know or witness of me is my imperfection. Imperfection is an intimate vulnerability—one I instinctively seek to hide.

I have lived my whole life needing to be perfect, striving so desperately hard with all my strength to be perfect in every single way. I have tried to be the perfect wife, daughter, sister, mother, and friend.

In business I have endlessly held myself up to the standard of being the perfect employee, leader, entrepreneur, executive assistant, and writer. Finances, relationships, career, physical appearance, lifestyle—in all these areas, anything less than absolute 100% perfection has felt like crushingly abject failure that I must hide from everyone.

Part of this is simply my nature, but nurture played a role as well. The nurture root of this intense focus on perfection started when I was a young child and an A- wasn't good enough. It found ample water and fertilizer in the Sunday morning messages of legalistic pastors preaching an unattainable blend of gospel and law. Their words insinuated that although Jesus had paid the price for our sins, we still must show evidence of our rebirth by living perfectly as Christ had lived.

It's ironic that the one place above all others where I should have received the message that I was not in fact expected to be able to attain perfection on my own was a place where I often saw the veneer of striving perfection demonstrated most.

The ongoing existence of Christian sin is an imperfection the culture of my childhood church failed to acknowledge, validate, and normalize. Although pastors would sometimes talk about sins from their distant past, they tended to be much less forthcoming about current struggles and temptations.

As leaders of the church, I understand they wanted to set good examples for the rest of us. Unfortunately, their collective example did not seem to include acknowledging the inevitable reality of their own failures as much as it did disparagingly pointing out and warning against such shortcomings in others.

We followed all the "rules," and any rules we weren't following, we discretely swept under the rug to maintain our thin veneer of perfection. We were like cats quietly yet frantically scrambling behind the scenes to cover up the evidence and stench of poop while blaming any lingering odor on the dog.

We were Christians, after all, and Christians were supposed to live perfectly like Christ who didn't sin. Except, of course, we did. We sinned, and then we layered a heaping dose of pride and ego or guilt and shame atop the original mistake. Such was the culmination of our overscrupulous, legalistic, extrinsically driven striving perfectionism.

It was from atop this unacknowledged dung heap that we cast stones of judgement at others. Or at least that is the message I internalized and lived out myself during my time in the fundamentalist church.

CHAPTER 17
SAFE TO BE IMPERFECT

By the time I became an adult, pietism and perfectionism had blossomed into the toxic flowers of risk aversion and self-limiting beliefs. Imagine how few new skills you are willing to learn if you believe you must be perfect right away and you view your inevitable mistakes as horrifically unacceptable failures rather than merely expected stops on the learning curve to mastery.

In my reality, the stakes of imperfection have always been high, and unfortunately imperfection could crop up anywhere. In high school, for example, if I wasn't first chair clarinet in band, it didn't merely mean Beth had performed better in the tryouts, it indicated to others I wasn't perfect. When my marriage to Rob officially ended, I held the decree of divorce in my hands. There it was—a signed, sealed, court-authenticated proof of my failure at keeping the weightiest promise I had ever made.

In my mind, if I wasn't perfect, I wasn't valuable. If I wasn't valuable, I wasn't lovable. If I wasn't lovable, then I stood condemned and alone. Imperfection was dangerous and potentially eternally fatal.

Although I don't remember hearing the doctrine of perfect, sinless Christianity preached specifically, I wonder if the cultural norm came from verses like 1 John 3:9 which when read individually and interpreted legalistically sounds as though if anyone ever sins, they are not saved. "Whosoever is born of God doth not commit sin; for his seed remaineth in him: and he cannot sin, because he is born of God" (1 John 3:9).

Clearly the legalistic understanding of this verse is lacking, however, because just one chapter earlier, in 1 John 2:1-2, John encourages us with the reminder that, "if any man sin, we have an advocate with the Father, Jesus Christ the righteous: and he is the propitiation for our sins…"

Paul also attests to the existence of Christian sin and imperfection in Romans 7:19 when he vulnerably shares, "For the good that I would I do not: but the evil which I would not, that I do." Though Paul's spirit has been renewed and he wants to do good, he still falls short and stumbles.

The apostle Paul was not perfect, yet unlike many fundamentalists, Paul openly shared the reality of his ongoing flaws for other Christians to read and draw encouragement from. Somehow, he seems to have felt safe acknowledging his inability to be perfect.

Perfect Impossibility

In Matthew 5:17, 18, and 20 Jesus says, "Think not that I am come to destroy the law, or the prophets: I am not come to destroy, but to fulfil. For verily I say unto you,

Till heaven and earth pass, one jot or one tittle shall in no wise pass from the law, till all be fulfilled...For I say unto you, That except your righteousness shall exceed the righteousness of the scribes and Pharisees, ye shall in no case enter into the kingdom of heaven."

Jesus didn't come to get rid of the law and say we should just try our best to be "good" people instead. If that were the case, we would be left anxiously hoping that we've somehow met the ambiguous and unknown achievement threshold for making it into Heaven.

No, the act of Jesus coming to Earth, living a sinless life, and being crucified was in fact a plan put into action precisely because the entry standards for Heaven *didn't* change and were never going to change. From the Old Testament to the New Testament to today, the standard has always been perfection. Jesus didn't abolish that standard—he met it and then offered those who came to him the ability to be credited with his perfection.

Understood from a non-legalistic standpoint, Jesus' words in Matthew 5:20 would have painted a very clear picture for the original audience. The gathered crowd would have been intimately familiar with the "righteousness" of the Pharisees. Jesus' audience knew the Pharisees did everything possible to follow each "jot and tittle" of biblical law and of all the extra laws they created to supplement it.

If *anyone* could get to Heaven by righteousness, it would have been the Pharisees. Saying that one's righteousness must *exceed* that of the Pharisees to earn a ticket to Heaven was intentionally preposterous. Jesus' audience would have known such a feat was not possible, so they would have correctly understood the message to be one of pointing away from works-based justification and toward the need for another path to God.

Thanks to my legalistic baggage, however, my pietistic mind had read these verses as a mandate to try harder. The law was there and there to stay which meant I must obey it. Perfectly.

The Need for a Physician

The reality is, John knew we would fail; Paul knew we would fall short; Jesus and God knew we would make mistakes. They all understood we would forever be imperfect while on this planet. Still, even with all the proof that I was flawed, I continued to think perfection was the standard and anything less must be hidden.

It took me a while to realize that by believing the goal from Matthew 9:11-13 and Mark 2:16-17 was to be perfect and have no need for a physician, I was in fact perpetuating the mistakes of the Pharisees who viewed themselves as "whole."

The point wasn't to be healthy and perfect all on my own. The point was to realize and accept that none of us are. Contrary to what I used to believe, in these passages Jesus wasn't saying that the Pharisees weren't "sick." He was saying that everyone is "sick," but only those who recognize it, acknowledge it, and go to the doctor to seek treatment can be made well.

"The righteous have no need for a physician" is like saying the chronic heavy drinker who denies he has a problem has no need for rehab. Truthfully, rehab is *exactly* what this person needs, but until a person wants to change, they will not. It is the alcoholic who acknowledges his situation and seeks treatment who will get that supportive care.

The Pharisees saw no need to change, so in their righteous eyes, they were "whole" and "need[ed] not a physician." These verses showed me that instead of promoting the self-conscious hiding of my flaws, Jesus was in fact creating a safe place for me to bring him my imperfections. He was lovingly waiting to help fix my mess if I would just hand it to him instead of hiding it.

CHAPTER 18
FORGIVEN IMPERFECTION

Once we recognize our imperfections, take responsibility for the mistakes, then ask for and receive healing forgiveness, we must move on. It is time to leave the guilt and pain of the past in the past.

Unlike Lot's wife who turned to look back at the city she came from and was forever frozen in that backward gaze, we must avoid the urge to fixate on the failures of our former lives.

Those of us with a sensitive conscience, conditioned by pietism sometimes need the reminder Shannon gave me to let go of the guilt and shame by finding a way to authentically apologize to ourselves as well.

Don't look back, or you will be destroyed, I remind myself. *Once you leave that old life behind, don't return to it. Don't longingly look back at it or guiltily ruminate about it. Don't spend time and energy focused on anything to do with it, lest it consume you. It is in the past, and God has come to fully rescue and redeem you from it if you choose to let him.*

What Shannon said about owning the wrongness echoed what Mark has told me for years about any sort of mess-ups in life: "Own it and move on." In this case, "Forgive yourself and move on." What God has declared forgiven is forgiven indeed. It's done. It's over with. We help no one by dwelling on it. If we keep looking back on our failures, we will merely be destroyed.

Live Up to It

The idea of owning our mistakes, asking for forgiveness, forgiving ourselves, and then moving on even when we stumble was illustrated beautifully through a story arc in Season 2 of *The Chosen*, a multi-season TV series about Jesus from the perspective of his disciples.

In Season 1, Episode 1 of *The Chosen*, while Mary Magdelene was possessed by demons, she was shown getting drunk, gambling heavily, and prostituting herself with Roman soldiers until Jesus rescued and redeemed her. He found her in a bar and followed her outside where he lovingly took her into his arms, declaring, "Thus says the Lord who created you, and He who formed you: Fear not, for I have redeemed you; I have called you by your name; You are mine."

Mary had memorized Isaiah 43:1 as a child and had repeated those words over and over in times of fear, but when Jesus spoke them to her, suddenly they become so very personal and real. She recognized Jesus as God and trusted him to redeem her.

During Season 2 Episode 5, Mary is shown memorizing and reciting Bible verses that she can draw strength from in times of trial. Then she encounters Roman soldiers and is confronted by a man possessed by the same demons who used to be in her. Mary tries to hold onto the strength of her faith, but ultimately, she hides from the soldiers and is unnerved by the demons. Triggered by her past and consumed by feelings of failure and guilt, Mary runs to the nearby town where she is drawn back into the familiarity of her old coping mechanisms.

In Episode 6, two of the disciples find Mary and convince her to return to the camp where Jesus is waiting to speak with her.

"I'm so ashamed. You redeemed me, and I just threw it all away," Mary says of her missteps.

"Well, that's not much of a redemption if it can be lost in a day, is it?" Jesus counters.

"I owe you everything. I just don't think I can do it."

"Do what?"

"Live up to it...I just can't live up to it."

"Well, that's true, but you don't have to. I just want your heart. The Father just wants your heart. Give us that, which you already have. The rest will come in time. Did you really think you would never struggle or sin again? I know how painful that moment was for you."

"I shouldn't."

"Someday. But not here...Look at me. I forgive you. It's over."[21]

Apparently, some believers took great offense to this exchange because it depicted someone close to Jesus falling and sinning even after redemption. For me, the conversation beautifully and poignantly illustrates the important distinction between justification and sanctification. It gives hope to recovering perfectionists. It reminds me of all the love and compassion Jesus has for my human failings.

The moment Mary recognized Jesus as God and trusted him to save her, she was justified and reconciled with God. She was declared perfect in God's eyes even though she herself was still flawed. Does that mean that she would never stumble and fall again? Did her justification mean that she would immediately become 100% perfect and righteous just like Jesus? No. That is where sanctification comes in.

Declared Lovable

Recovering perfectionists like myself must remember sanctification is called a process for a reason. Like Mary, I too will spend the rest of my life stumbling, failing, growing, and spiritually developing over time. No matter how much I may try to "live up to it" and follow the apparent mandate to "Be ye therefore perfect, even as your Father which is in heaven is perfect" (Matthew 5:48), I cannot wholly succeed.

That sounds depressing, but here is a beautiful, gloriously amazing truth that legalism never prepared me for: We do not have to be perfect to be loved. We are not expected to be perfect to be declared worthy.

My perfection was never expected. It was required, yes, but my very incapacity to meet the required level of perfection was already planned for. God sent Jesus long before I was ever on this planet continuing the human legacy of falling short. God knew I would fail, and not just before he redeemed me, but after too. My words and actions will not always reflect the heart of God, yet that does not mean I cease to be his child.

No matter what legalists may preach, the good news of the gospel isn't that humans are given salvation if we continually live up to it. That would be horrible news because we would all fail.

The good news is once we have accepted, trusted, and allowed Jesus to redeem us, we are secure in that redemption no matter how imperfect our attempts at following him. If our hearts are in the right place, the rest will come in time.

This means we are safe to do as Shannon said, to own that we were wrong and forgive ourselves for that wrongness so we can be free of the guilt and shame of failure. We can finally issue that authentic apology to self. Jesus has made it safe and provided a way for our lingering imperfections to be covered.

Acceptance

It took about three years, but with a lot of grace, truth, and love I believe I've finally worked through those five stages of grief and arrived at acceptance. The best part is, as it turns out, acceptance did not mean capitulation and a return to the world of legalistic, pietistic fundamentalism. It is so much better than that.

I am imperfect, yet so very loved. The one perfect being in the whole universe already planned for and personally covered my past, present, and future imperfections.

I have made and will continue to make mistakes, but I can forgive myself for that "wrongness."

I can rest secure in the knowledge that I don't have to pretend to be perfect to prove to God or anyone else that I am his daughter.

Jesus was perfect since I cannot be, and he gives me credit for his perfection out of love.

It is finished.

Acceptance.

Reflection Invite: Part 6

1. If I have felt like I needed to be perfect, it was because

    _____

    _____

    _____

    _____

    _____

    _____.

2. Acknowledging my inability to be perfect would mean

    _____

    _____

    _____

    _____

    _____

    _____.

3. My spiritual mistakes, regrets, and imperfections have
    taught me _____

    _____

    _____

    _____

    _____

    _____.

4. If I created my own barriers that have kept me from truth, they include _____

_____

_____

_____

_____

_____.

5. I can overcome those barriers now by _____

_____

_____

_____

_____

_____.

6. If I have gone through a spiritual or religious grieving process, and have now arrived at acceptance, I would describe acceptance as _____

_____

_____

_____.

7. If I have not yet arrived at acceptance, I imagine it will look like _____

_____

_____

_____.

EPILOGUE

I do not at all understand the mystery of grace—
only that it meets us where we are but
does not leave us where it found us.

—*Anne Lamott*

ABIDING IN GRACE

It was about love. In the end, it was always about love—the realization and acceptance of a grace-filled love I had lost all hope of experiencing. This redemptive love was stronger than guilt, shame, and ego. It had the power to obliterate decades of mistakes and failures. It was the fulfilled promise of the "perfect love" which "casts out fear" (1 John 4:18). It was beautiful, indescribable, and finally mine to have and to hold.

It still surprises me that I am at a place in my journey to have favorite Bible verses, but one that resonates very deeply with me is Jeremiah 29:13: "And ye shall seek me, and find me, when ye shall search for me with all your heart."

God revealed himself to me when I sought him with my whole heart. At the time, I would not have even said I was seeking God because I didn't believe he existed. What I *was* searching for was truth. I was whole heartedly seeking truth and had committed to following that truth wherever it led me. I just never expected it would lead me to God.

. . .

It is time. You've heard my story and followed my experiences. Now it's your turn. I invite you on your own journey to face the past, to break through barriers, to seek truth, love, and healing.

I am not saying you must go to church, read the Bible, or jump back into a version of the world that harmed you and whose scars you still bear. You will know when and if you're ready for any of that.

What I *am* inviting and encouraging you to do is to continue seeking and following truth in as unbiased a way as possible. Ask questions and dig for the answers rather than allowing others to impose them on you.

As Jonathan Roumie who plays Jesus on *The Chosen* said, "You've got nothing to lose to explore. As you get closer and closer, you'll know what's true."

I will leave you with the words of poet T.S. Eliot: "We shall never cease from exploration, and the end [purpose/goal] of all our exploring will be to arrive where we started and know the place for the first time."

Reflection Invite: Epilogue

1. If my spiritual beliefs have changed along this journey, I used to believe _____
   _____ ,
   but now I believe _____
   _____
   _____ .

2. The next step in my spiritual journey is to _____
   _____
   _____ .

3. I now feel _____
   about my spiritual and religious past.

4. I feel _____
   about my current and future spiritual life.

5. The greatest gift I have received because of having walked through this difficult spiritual journey is
   _____
   _____
   _____
   _____
   _____ .

ACKNOWLEDGMENTS

Mom and Dad: Parenting is an intimidating, uncharted lifelong journey with many opportunities to inadvertently hurt the children you love so dearly. It takes a great deal of bravery and boldness to choose such a role.

Even more courage is required not only to be supportive of your child writing a book like this one but also to choose to share and recommend the book to others as you have done.

The spiritual part of my childhood may have been rough, but for every painful memory, I have so many other joyous ones. I remember special holiday traditions, one-of-a-kind themed birthday parties with amazing homemade cake creations, the best DIY 4th of July parade costumes, moonlight ice skating and cross-country skiing, a trip to Boston to meet Sally Ride, and so much more.

Thank you for all these beautiful memories and for understanding why I needed to write this book even when it means sharing the imperfect moments for others to read and learn from.

• • •

Karen: You show that it's possible to grow up in fundamentalism, legalism, and pietism without internalizing it yourself. I admire your discernment and strength. Thank you for being a beta reader and sounding board for this book as it initially came together. I love you.

• • •

Mary: Just when I was feeling overwhelmed by all the finishing touches needed to get this book sent in, you showed up. As someone who also has been wounded by fundamentalist religion, you understand this topic so well. You spent hours talking with me and helping me find the right words to introduce this story and this journey to my readers. Thank you!

• • •

Matt: I didn't feel ready or qualified to become a stepmom, but you have always been so patient. I could not have asked for a more fantastic stepson.

Thank you for doing my author photoshoot, helping with my cover design, creating my trailer video, and forgiving me for throwing something at your face all those years ago. I am so blessed and honored to call you family.

• • •

Kary & Jeff: First living and then writing about my spiritual journey was a challenge. Finally submitting this book to publish and share with the world has in some ways been nearly as difficult. Thank you for being the support and recovering perfectionist accountability team I didn't know I needed.

• • •

Shannon: When I was stuck, you showed me the next steps and illuminated the way out. Thank you for allowing me to share your words and to shine that light for others who may also be trapped in the quicksand of ego and an inability to forgive themselves.

• • •

Mr. Steven Boyd: You were the first person to genuinely encourage me to ask the big questions. You were never intimidated or threatened by my need for understanding. You showed me how to seek and follow truth. Because of that—because of you—my life is infinitely richer and more rewarding. Thank you. I wish you were still here to read the book and see the life your mentorship helped create.

• • •

Beth: This journey has been long, and you have stood by me through it all. You have loved me as I am our whole lives, no strings attached. You are a beautiful woman and a wonderful friend. Thank you for being a part of this story and supporting me always as I worked to process and write it. I am so blessed by your continued presence in my life.

• • •

Mark: You too have walked by my side on this journey, and I cherish the depth and the many facets of our connectedness. You are my mentor, my husband, my lover, my friend, and my partner on all our many varied life adventures. There is no one I would rather walk this path with than you. "No measure of time with you will be long enough, but we'll start with forever."[22]

• • •

Elohim: Without you, this book and this story would never have come to pass, much less be written down for others to read. Thank you for your patience through all the many rounds of edits and revisions as you continued to reveal the parts that were not as they should be.

I recognize the finished work is still far from perfect, yet thankfully your truth does not depend upon my human attempts at unattainable perfection. Your unfailing grace-filled love, light, and forgiveness hold the power to drive out all darkness. Help me dwell in that light and radiate it always.

Thank you for the blessing of this marriage to Mark, who I believe is the husband you had planned for me all along. Thank you for saving this blessing for me even though I was not patient enough to wait for it from the beginning.

Thank you for staying with me and protecting me thorough all the mistakes and imperfections of my past to bring me to this moment, to your loving redemption. Thank you for working and continuing to work all things for good.

RECOMMENDED READING

The books on this list cover a full spectrum of Christian authors from conservative to progressive. Many authors have personally experienced the impact of legalism and harmful doctrine. Some, like me, spent part of their lives as atheists.

Each book on this list was chosen not because I necessarily agree 100% with all the author's views, but because I have either personally read it and found it helpful or because it has come highly recommended to me.

- Anderson, Neil. *Breaking the Bondage of Legalism* (Oregon: Harvest House Publishers, 2003).

- Baker, Connie. *Traumatized by Religious Abuse: Courage, Hope and Freedom for Survivors* (Luminare Press, LLC, 2019).

- Campbell, Susan. *Dating Jesus: A Story of Fundamentalism, Feminism, and the American Girl* (Boston: Beacon Press, 2009).

- Crafton, Barbara. *Jesus Wept: When Faith and Depression Meet* (Minneapolis: Fortress Press, 2019).
- Done, Dominic. *When Faith Fails: Finding God in the Shadow of Doubt* (Nashville: Thomas Nelson, 2019).
- Duggar Vuolo, Jinger. *Becoming Free Indeed: My Story of Disentangling Faith from Fear* (Nashville: Thomas Nelson, 2023)
- Gregoire, Sheila Wray. *The Good Girl's Guide to Great Sex: Creating a Marriage That's Both Holy and Hot* (Grand Rapids: Zondervan, 2022).
- Gregoire, Sheila Wray; Lindenbach, Rebecca Gregoire; Sawatsky, Joanna. *The Great Sex Rescue: The Lies You've Been Taught and How to Recover What God Intended* (Ada: Baker Books, 2021).
- Gutherie, Nancy. *The One Year Book of Discovering Jesus in the Old Testament* (Carol Stream: Tyndale Momentum, 2010).
- Held Evans, Rachel. *Faith Unraveled: How a Girl Who Knew All the Answers Learned to Ask Questions* (Grand Rapids: Zondervan, 2010).
- Lewis, C.S. *Mere Christianity* (HarperOne, 2015).
- McDowell, Josh. *More Than a Carpenter* (Carol Stream: Tyndale Momentum, 2009).
- McGrath, Alister. *Mere Apologetics: How to Help Seekers and Skeptics Find Faith* (Ada: Baker Books, 2012).
- McHargue, Mike. *Finding God in the Waves: How I Lost My Faith and Found It Again Through Science* (New York: Convergent Books, 2017).
- Merritt, Carol Howard. *Healing Spiritual Wounds: Reconnecting with a Loving God After Experiencing a Hurtful Church* (San Francisco: HarperOne, 2017).

- O'Connell, Michael. *Finding God in Science: The Extraordinary Evidence For The Soul And Christianity, A Rocket Scientist's Gripping Odyssey* (Eigen Publishing, 2018).

- Oberbrunner, Kary. *Your Secret Name: An Uncommon Quest to Stop Pretending, Shed the Labels, and Discover Your True Identity* (Ohio: Author Academy Elite, 2018).

- Pasquale, Teresa. *Sacred Wounds: A Path to Healing from Spiritual Trauma* (Nashville: Chalice Press, 2015)

- Phelps-Roper, Megan. *Unfollow: A Memoir of Loving and Leaving Extremism* (London: Picador, 2020).

- Phillips, J.B., *Your God is Too Small: A Guide for Believers and Skeptics Alike* (New York: Touchstone, 2004)

- Ripken, Nik. *The Insanity of God: A True Story of Faith Resurrected* (Nashville: B&H Books, 2013).

- Theocast Inc. *Rest: a consideration of faith vs. faithfulness* (Independently Published, 2021).

- Theocast Inc. *Safe in Christ: A Primer On Assurance* (Independently Published, 2020).

- Tozer, A.W. *The Pursuit of God: Updated Edition* (Abbotsford: Aneko Press, 2015).

- Warner Wallace, J. *Cold-Case Christianity: A Homicide Detective Investigates the Claims of the Gospels* (Colorado Springs: David C. Cook, 2013).

- Wilson, Ian. *The Blood and the Shroud: New Evidence that the World's Most Sacred Relic is Real* (New York: Free Press, 1999).

ENDNOTES

1 In fundamentalist Baptist churches, the old King James Version of the Bible is often considered to be the only truly accurate English language version. For this reason, the verses I memorized as a child were KJV, and I maintain the use of that version here.

2 Olga Khazan, "What Time of Day Do We Feel Most Anxious?" *The Atlantic*, September 10, 2014, https://www.theatlantic.com/health/archive/2014/09/when-do-we-feel-bad/379586/.

3 Moffitt, J. & Perdue, J (Hosts). (2019-Present). *Theocast* [Audio Podcast]. https://theocast.org/.

4 Josh McDowell, *Why True Love Waits; The Definitive Book on How to Help Your Kids Resist Sexual Pressure* (Carol Stream, IL: Tyndale House Publishers, Inc., 2002).

5 Joshua Harris, *I Kissed Dating Goodbye: A New Attitude Toward Relationships and Romance* (Colorado Springs, CO: Multnomah Books, 1997).

6   Wells, Steve, *The Skeptic's Annotated Bible*, (Moscow, ID: SAB Books, LLC, 2013).

7   Gregoire, Sheila Wray; Lindenbach, Rebecca Gregoire; Sawatsky, Joanna. *The Great Sex Rescue: The Lies You've Been Taught and How to Recover What God Intended* (Ada: Baker Books, 2021).

8   https://www.beliefnet.com/entertainment/quizzes/test/beliefomatic.aspx.

9   "The Argument from Locality," *Daylight Atheism (blog)*, Patheos (January 23, 2021), https://www.patheos.com/blogs/daylightatheism/essays/the-argument-from-locality/.

10   Frank Lorey, M.A., "The Flood of Noah and the Flood of Gilgamesh," *Institute for Creation Research* (March 1, 1997), https://www.icr.org/article/noah-flood-gilgamesh/.

11   David Wright, "Timeline for the Flood," *Answers In Genesis* (March 9, 2012), https://www.answersingenesis.org/bible-timeline/timeline-for-the-flood/.

12   Carlos Baker, *Ernest Hemingway: Selected Letters 1917-1961* (Granada: St. Albans & London, 1981)

13   Alyson M. Stone, "Thou Shalt Not: Treating Religious Trauma and Spiritual Harm With Combined Therapy," *Semantic Scholar*, Group, Vol. 37, No. 4 (Winter 2013), https://www.semanticscholar.org/paper/Thou-Shalt-Not%3A-Treating-Religious-Trauma-and-Harm-Stone/b7e7e20b45fa8a6c8aa082468c1ca4fec010e59d.

14   Susan Campbell, *Dating Jesus: A Story of Fundamentalism, Feminism, and the American Girl*. (Boston, MA: Beacon Press, 2009).

15   Steve Smith, "'Crock-Pot' Trauma: Spiritual Abuse and Recovery," *Liberty for Captives* (October 4, 2012), https://www.libertyforcaptives.com/2012/10/04/crock-pot-trauma-spiritual-abuse-and-recovery/.

16 Marlene Winell, "Religious Trauma Syndrome." *Journey Free: Recovery from Harmful Religion* (March 13, 2021), https://www.journeyfree.org/rts/.

17 *A Lucasfilm Ltd. Production released by Twentieth Century Fox Film Corporation, written and directed by George Lucas; produced by Rick McCallum. Star Wars. Episode I, The Phantom Menace. Beverly Hills, Calif.: Twentieth Century Fox Home Entertainment, 2013.*

18 "Hate," Def. 1, *Merriam-Webster* (March 14, 2021), https://www.merriam-webster.com/dictionary/hate, n.d. Web.

19 Elisabeth Kübler-Ross, M.D. and David Kessler, *On Grief and Grieving: Finding the Meaning of Grief Through the Five Stages of Loss* (New York, NY: Scribner, 2005).

20 "Commune," Def. 1 and 2. *Dictionary.com* (March 14, 2021), https://www.dictionary.com/browse/commune, n.d. Web.

21 *Jenkins, Dallas, dir. "Unlawful." The Chosen, season 2, episode 6, Angel Studios, 2021.*

22 *Summit Entertainment presents a Temple Hill production in association with Sunswept Entertainment; produced by Wyck Godfrey, Karen Rosenfelt, Stephanie Meyer; screenplay by Melissa Rosenberg; directed by Bill Condon. The Twilight Saga. Breaking Dawn, Part 1. Universal City, CA :Summit Entertainment, 2012.*

ABOUT THE AUTHOR

Susan Ford is an author, coach, and former fundamentalist Baptist. She offers those harmed by religion a safe place to ask questions and explore answers so they can find truth and experience healing. Susan loves traveling the world while doing meaningful work and creating lasting memories alongside her husband, Mark.

Connect with Susan at susanford.com

  @susanmarieford

 @susan.marie.ford

Made in the USA
Coppell, TX
07 December 2022

88090784R00152